Studies on the Haggadah

FROM THE TEACHINGS OF
NECHAMA LEIBOWITZ

הגדת נחמה

edited by

Yitshak Reiner and Shmuel Peerless

URIM PUBLICATIONS
New York • Jerusalem

Studies on the Haggadah: From the Teachings of Nechama Leibowitz
edited by Yitshak Reiner and Shmuel Peerless
Copyright © 2002 by Yitshak Reiner and Shmuel Peerless

First Edition
ISBN 965-7108-38-1

Urim Publications, P.O. BOX 52287, Jerusalem 91521 Israel

Lambda Publishers Inc.
3709 13th Avenue Brooklyn, New York 11218 U.S.A.
Tel: 718-972-5449 Fax: 718-972-6307
E-mail: mh@ejudaica.com

www.UrimPublications.com

Designed by Raphaël Freeman, Jerusalem
Typeset by Jerusalem Typesetting, www.jerusalemtype.com

Introduction

והגדת לבנך ביום ההוא.... (שמות יג:ח)

And you shall tell your children on that day.... (Shemot 13:8)

THE RABBIS who edited the Haggadah understood that the story could not just be told, but had to be transmitted in such a way that the participants of the Seder would internalize its message. The Haggadah, therefore, presents a unique experiential educational program that includes music, drama, and the use of the various senses. But the essence of the educational approach reflected in the Haggadah is the question and answer method. Many of the Seder rituals and visual aids are designed to motivate the children present to ask questions. The Maggid section of the Haggadah therefore begins with the four questions. The Gemara (*Pesachim* 116a) states that even if there is not a child present who can ask the question, the adult participants must ask the questions. In fact, even if present at the Seder are only two scholars who are well-versed in the laws of Pesach, they must still ask each other the questions. The Rabbis understood that the effectiveness of an educational experience is greatly enhanced when the participants are actively engaged in the learning process, and are not mere passive recipients of information.

Nechama Leibowitz was among the outstanding Torah scholars and teachers of our generation. Her unique instructional methods are utilized by many Torah teachers throughout the world today. Nechama's method is based on the principle of active learning. The cornerstone of her approach is the presentation of questions on the biblical text and relevant commentaries that require the learner to independently analyze and draw conclusions. Over a thirty-year period, Nechama prepared *Gilyonot* (study sheets) on the weekly Torah portion that presented textual comparisons, stylistic literary analyses and commentaries with probing questions designed to foster in-depth study of the sources.

Nechama's approach to Torah study is thus very compatible with the methodology reflected in the Haggadah. As such, it is helpful and challenging to apply Nechama's work to the Pesach Seder. This Haggadah collects questions relating to the Seder from Nechama's *Gilyonot* and other writings, and organizes them according to the text of the Haggadah. It includes questions on the text of the Haggadah itself as well as the biblical verses on which the Haggadah is based. Selected commentaries and questions on their interpretations are also included. Our "suggested answers" to Nechama's questions are provided. We say "suggested answers" because it is quite possible that in the course of the readers' own analysis and discussion, alternative answers may arise. The purpose of this Haggadah is to enable individuals and families to engage in a meaningful study of the story of the Exodus from Egypt before, during, and after the Seder night experience.

וכל המרבה לספר ביציאת מצרים הרי זה משובח.

And anyone who increases the telling of the story of the
Exodus from Egypt is praiseworthy. (Haggadah)

יצחק ריינר
שמואל פירלס

ירושלים עיה״ק, תשס״ב

EDITORS' NOTE: All of the supplementary sources utilized in this Haggadah are taken from the teachings and writings of Nechama Leibowitz. The vast majority of the questions presented are drawn directly from Nechama's *Gilyonot*, but some are taken from her other writings, lectures or personal conversations. A few additional questions in Nechama's style have also been added to connect the sources brought by Nechama to the text of the Haggadah. For those interested in knowing the source of each question, a detailed list is provided at the back of the book. Also provided is brief biographical information on the commentators mentioned in this Haggadah. The annotation of footnotes are the contribution of the editors.

In Nechama's pedagogical approach, she recognized the necessity of providing challenges for students of varying levels, and accordingly presented questions (in her *Gilyonot*) in a graded fashion. This methodology is likewise reflected in this Haggadah, with the use of symbols to indicate levels of difficulty: with one kiddush cup ⚱ designating a more difficult question, and two kiddush cups ⚱⚱ designating an even greater level of difficulty.

ACKNOWLEDGMENTS

A few of the *Gilyonot* utilized in this work have been published in recent years, with suggested answers by Yitshak Reiner, under the auspices of the Jewish National Fund and the World Council for Torah Education. Many of the questions in the Haggadah are also discussed in Nechama's *Studies in Parshat Hashavua*, published by the World Zionist Organization. We recommend these resources for those who wish to delve more deeply into the teachings of Nechama Leibowitz.

Finally, we would like to express our appreciation to Rabbi Mordechai Spiegelman, Marla Frankel and Shira Leibowitz Schmidt for their help in the review and final editing of this work. We would also like to thank Sorelle Wachmann of Urim Publications for her valuable editorial input.

"A Night of Vigil" – ליל שמורים

The first night of Pesach has a special status in the Torah. It is designated as "a night of vigil" ("leil shimurim"–ליל שמורים) for Bnai Yisrael throughout the generations:

לֵיל שִׁמֻּרִים הוּא לַה׳ לְהוֹצִיאָם מֵאֶרֶץ מִצְרַיִם הוּא הַלַּיְלָה הַזֶּה לה׳ שִׁמֻּרִים לְכָל בְּנֵי יִשְׂרָאֵל לְדֹרֹתָם.

(שמות יב:מב)

It is a night of vigil to the Lord for bringing them out of the land of Egypt; this is the Lord's night, a night of vigil for all of Bnai Yisrael for their generations. (Shemot 12:42)

The following are two explanations of this difficult verse:

RAMBAN: [The Torah] refers to it as "a night of vigil for bringing them out of the land of Egypt" because from the time that he decreed the exile [in Egypt], God kept in mind ("shamar"–שמר) that he would redeem them on that very night... or because he waited ("shamar"–שמר) in anticipation of the day that he would bring them out of Egypt, that is that God waited until the time that they would be worthy of redemption.... And the meaning of the phrase "this is the Lord's night, a night of vigil for all of Bnai Yisrael for

their generations" is that this night is for God, that is sanctified to His name.... That they [Bnai Yisrael] should observe it by serving Him through the eating of the Pesach offering, remembering the miracles, and offering praise and thanks.

KLI YAKAR: [the Torah] states "it is a night of vigil to the Lord" and then it states: "a night of vigil for all of Bnai Yisrael for their generations" because God said to Bnai Yisrael: "My flame is in your hands and your flame is in my hand. You protect me and I will protect you".... And behold on that night, Bnai Yisrael kept the flame [of God] by diligently observing the mitzvah of the Pesach offering, and God protected them by not allowing the destruction to affect their homes.

Questions
1) What is the difference between Ramban's two interpretations on the phrase "it is a night of vigil to the Lord"?
2) How is Ramban's interpretation of the verse different from that of the Kli Yakar's, and how is it similiar?

Suggested Answers
1) According to Ramban's first interpretation, the day on which Bnai Yisrael would be redeemed from Egypt was set 400 years

earlier, and would be fulfilled regardless of their merit. According to his second interpretation, the redemption was based on the merit of *Bnai Yisrael*, even before the previously appointed time.

2) Ramban and the *Kli Yakar* disagree both on the meaning of the word "*shimurim*" (שמורים) in the phrase "a night of vigil for bringing them out of the land of Egypt," and on its object. *Ramban* translates the word as either "kept in mind" or "waited in anticipation." In both cases, the object is the night (i.e., God kept this night in mind or God waited for this night). The *Kli Yakar* translates the word as "guarding," in the sense of protecting. In his interpretation, the object is

Bnai Yisrael who were protected on that night by God.

Ramban and the *Kli Yakar* agree that the word "*shimurim*" in the latter phrase "a night of vigil for all of *Bnai Yisrael* for their generations" means "observance" and refers to the observance of the rituals of the *Seder*. Here too, however, there is a subtle difference in their interpretations. According to *Ramban*, our observance of the *Seder* is an ongoing gesture of recognition and appreciation of God for His redemption of our ancestors. According to the *Kli Yakar*, the Seder is an ongoing manifestation of our reciprocal "protection" of God by helping to maintain the "flame of Torah" in the world.

The Four Cups – ארבע כוסות

THE FOUR EXPRESSIONS OF REDEMPTION

The *Talmud Yerushalmi* (*Pesachim* 10a) informs us that the four cups that we drink at the Seder are based on the four expressions of redemption that are found at the beginning of *parashat Va'era* (*Shemot* 6:6–8):

לכן אמור לבני ישראל: אני ה'. והוצאתי אתכם מתחת סבלות מצרים, והצלתי אתכם מעבדתם, וגאלתי אתכם בזרוע נטויה ובשפטים גדולים. ולקחתי אתכם לי לעם והייתי לכם לאלהים, וידעתם כי אני ה' אלהיכם המוציא אתכם מתחת סבלות מצרים.

Say therefore to the *Bnai Yisrael*: I am the Lord. And *I will take you out* from under the burdens of Egypt, and *I will save you* from their bondage, and *I will redeem you* with an outstretched arm and with great judgments.

And *I will take you* to Me as a people [referring to the giving of the Torah at Mount Sinai] and I will be your God, and you shall know that I am the Lord your God who takes you out from under the burdens of Egypt.

8

Question

Explain the gradual change that is taking place from the first expression to the second, then to the third, and finally to the fourth.

Suggested Answer

The sequence of the four expressions of redemption reflects the changing relationship between *Bnai Yisrael* and both the Egyptians and God, as follows:

1) "And **I will take you out** from under the burdens of Egypt"—*Bnai Yisrael* are at this point under total subjugation to the Egyptians.

2) "And **I will save you** from their bondage"—Here the Egyptian bondage is still a factor, but the Egyptians are not mentioned by name. This reflects a lessening of the subjugation.

3) "And **I will redeem you**"—Here the Egyptians and the bondage are not referred to at all, reflecting a liberation from Egyptian subjugation.

4) "And **I will take you** to me as a people"—After being completely liberated from the Egyptians, *Bnai Yisrael* can forge a new relationship with God.

THE FIFTH EXPRESSION OF REDEMPTION

It has been noted that these promises are actually followed by a fifth expression of redemption, והבאתי—"And *I will bring* (you to the land...)." (*Shemot* 6:9)

והבאתי אתכם אל הארץ אשר נשאתי את ידי לתת אותה לאברהם ליצחק וליעקב.
And *I will bring you* to the land, concerning which I swore with an uplifted hand to give to Avraham, Yitzchak and Yaakov....

According to many commentators, this expression is reflected in the cup of Eliyahu. Why do we not drink the fifth cup?

The *Or Hachaim* also noted a textual difficulty in this section: Why is the consequence "and you shall know that I am the Lord your God" juxtaposed between the four promises (,והוצאתי, והצלתי, וגאלתי ולקחתי) and the fifth (והבאתי)? Should it not come at the conclusion of all of the promises? The following is his answer:

The statement "you shall know that I am the Lord your God" is deliberately placed before that of "I shall bring you to the land" to stress that this was the precondition for the fulfillment of the "I shall bring you to the land." Failing this [the acknowledgment of God], they would not enjoy the fulfillment of the subsequent promises.

Questions

1) How does the *Or Hachaim* solve the textual difficulty?

2) How does his solution diverge from the generally accepted meaning of the text?

Suggested Answers

1) The *Or Hachaim* suggests that the placement of this phrase indicates that recognition of God is a precondition for the fulfillment of the latter promise, the entry into *Eretz Yisrael*. In other words, the fulfillment of that aspect is not only dependent on God, but also on the faith and recognition demonstrated by *Bnai Yisrael*. Without this recognition, God would not fulfill the promise of entry into *Eretz Yisrael*.

2) This interpretation differs from the usual understanding of the expression, "and you shall know…," which seems to be a consequence of the promises. The *Or Hachaim* interprets it as a condition, rather than a consequence.

THE BOND BETWEEN GOD AND BNAI YISRAEL

There are those who solve the difficulty raised by the *Or Hachaim* in an alternative manner based on the famous dictum of R. Akiva in *Pirkei Avot* 3:14:

> He used to say: "Beloved is man that he was created in the image of God; but it was by a greater love that it was made known to him that he was created in the image of God."

Question

Why, according to this opinion, does the phrase "and you shall know that I am the Lord your God" come specifically where it does?

Suggested Answer

According to this explanation, the statement "and you shall know that I am the Lord your God" represents a blessing: the recognition of the special relationship between God and *Bnai Yisrael* which is reflected in the redemption from Egypt and the giving of the Torah at Mount Sinai. It is a special gift given by God rather than a condition placed on *Bnai Yisrael* before entering the land. According to Nechama, this recognition of God was the primary goal of the Exodus from Egypt and would give greater meaning and purpose to the entry into *Eretz Yisrael*.

WHY WE DRINK FOUR CUPS

Question

How do the above commentaries help to explain why we drink four rather than five cups of wine at the Seder?

Suggested Answer

Both of these commentaries demonstrate that the Torah text itself separates the first four expressions of redemption from the fifth expression (והבאתי) with the statement "and you shall know that I am the Lord your God."

According to the *Or Hachaim*, the statement creates a division between those aspects that are solely within God's purview, and those that require further involvement from *Bnai Yisrael*.

According to the second commentary, the placement of the phrase "and you shall know that I am the Lord your God" indicates that the fourth expression (ולקחתי—the giving of the Torah at Sinai and the subsequent recognition of God's relationship to *Bnai Yisrael*) represents the primary goal of the redemption from Egypt.*

Nechama herself explained that the fifth expression "והבאתי" is not reflected in a cup of wine at the Seder because, although the promise would be fulfilled, *Bnai Yisrael* would subsequently go into exile. While the impact of the first four promises was eternal, the fulfillment of the fifth would be interrupted. Nechama added that when the State of Israel was established, Rav Menachem Kasher (author of the תורה שלמה) tried unsuccessfully to convince the Rabbinate to institute a fifth cup.

---

* Interestingly, Rav Soloveitchik made a similar comment on the fact that the Mishna (*Pesachim* 10:4) requires that the Seder include a study of the section of the Torah that begins with ארמי אובד אבי (*Devarim* 26:5) "until he completes the entire section." He points out that the section actually ends with verse 9 that reads: "And he brought us (ויביאנו) to this place, and gave us this land: a land flowing with milk and honey." This verse, however, is not included in the text of the Haggadah. Just as the final expression of redemption (והבאתי) is not included in the cups of wine at the Seder, so too the final verse (ויביאנו) is excluded from the Haggadah. From this, Rav Soloveitchik similarly concluded that the giving of the Torah was the primary goal of the Exodus from Egypt, and a necessary step that would give meaning to entering *Eretz Yisrael*.

‫בְּדִיקַת חָמֵץ‬

The search for chametz begins upon nightfall of the fourteenth day of Nissan. We must search all areas where chametz may have been brought during the course of the year, even if a thorough clearning was done before Passover. The search should not be interrupted until its completion. If the Seder falls on Saturday night, the search is made on Thursday night. There is a custom to distribute ten pieces of chametz through the house prior to the search. Care should be taken to note the locations of these hidden pieces.

The following blessing is recited before the search for chametz:

‫בָּרוּךְ אַתָּה יְיָ אֱלֹהֵינוּ מֶלֶךְ הָעוֹלָם, אֲשֶׁר קִדְּשָׁנוּ בְּמִצְוֹתָיו,‬
‫וְצִוָּנוּ עַל בִּעוּר חָמֵץ.‬

After the search, one should wrap the chametz and put it in a safe place. Then, the following declaration is made. (The declaration must be understood in order to take effect. Any chametz that you still want to use is not included in the declaration.)

‫כָּל חֲמִירָא וַחֲמִיעָה דְּאִכָּא בִרְשׁוּתִי דְּלָא חֲמִתֵּהּ וּדְלָא‬
‫בִעַרְתֵּהּ וּדְלָא יְדַעְנָא לֵהּ לִבְטִיל וְלֶהֱוֵי הֶפְקֵר כְּעַפְרָא‬
‫דְאַרְעָא.‬

‫בִּעוּר חָמֵץ‬

On the morning after the search, before ten o'clock, we burn all existing chametz. The meaning of this declaration must be understood. If the Seder falls on Saturday night, this declaration is made on Shabbat morning; however, the burning takes place on Friday morning. Any chametz remaining from the Shabbat morning meal is to be flushed down the drain. After burning (or on Shabbat, flushing) the following declaration is made:

‫כָּל חֲמִירָא וַחֲמִיעָה דְּאִכָּא בִרְשׁוּתִי [דַּחֲזִתֵּהּ וּדְלָא חֲזִתֵּהּ],‬
‫דַּחֲמִתֵּהּ וּדְלָא חֲמִתֵּהּ, דְּבִעַרְתֵּהּ וּדְלָא בִעַרְתֵּהּ, לִיבְטִיל‬
‫וְלֶהֱוֵי [הֶפְקֵר] כְּעַפְרָא דְאַרְעָא.‬

ഔ *The Search for Chametz* ca

The search for chametz begins upon nightfall of the fourteenth day of Nissan. We must search all areas where chametz may have been brought during the course of the year, even if a thorough clearning was done before Passover. The search should not be interrupted until its completion. If the Seder falls on Saturday night, the search is made on Thursday night. There is a custom to distribute ten pieces of chametz through the house prior to the search. Care should be taken to note the locations of these hidden pieces.

The following blessing is recited before the search for chametz:

Blessed are You, Hashem, our God, King of the universe, Who has sanctified us with His commandments and has commanded us to remove all chametz from our possession.

After the search, one should wrap the chametz and put it in a safe place. Then, the following declaration is made. (The declaration must be understood in order to take effect. Any chametz that you still want to use is not included in the declaration.)

All leaven that is in my possession which I have not seen, have not removed and do not know about, should be as if it does not exist and should become ownerless, like the dust of the earth.

ഔ *Burning the Chametz* ca

On the morning after the search, before ten o'clock, we burn all existing chametz. The meaning of this declaration must be understood. If the Seder falls on Saturday night, this declaration is made on Shabbat morning; however, the burning takes place on Friday morning. Any chametz remaining from the Shabbat morning meal is to be flushed down the drain. After burning (or on Shabbat, flushing) the following declaration is made:

All leaven that is in my possession, whether I have seen it or not, which I have removed or not, should be as if it does not exist and should become ownerless, like the dust of the earth.

⊰ עֵרוּב תַּבְשִׁילִין ⊱

When Passover falls on Thursday, an *eiruv tavshilin* must be made on Wednesday for it to be permissible to cook on Yom Tov for Shabbat. The *eiruv* indicates that preparations for Shabbat have begun prior to Yom Tov. The head of the household takes some matzah and any cooked food and sets them aside until Shabbat, to be used on Shabbat. Then the following is recited:

בָּרוּךְ אַתָּה יְיָ אֱלֹהֵינוּ מֶלֶךְ הָעוֹלָם, אֲשֶׁר קִדְּשָׁנוּ בְּמִצְוֹתָיו, וְצִוָּנוּ עַל מִצְוַת עֵרוּב.

בַּהֲדֵין עֵרוּבָא יְהֵא שָׁרֵא לָנָא לַאֲפוּיֵי וּלְבַשּׁוּלֵי וּלְאַטְמוּנֵי וּלְאַדְלוּקֵי שְׁרָגָא וּלְתַקָּנָא וּלְמֶעְבַּד כָּל צָרְכָנָא, מִיּוֹמָא טָבָא לְשַׁבַּתָּא לָנוּ וּלְכָל יִשְׂרָאֵל הַדָּרִים בָּעִיר הַזֹּאת.

⊰ הַדְלָקַת נֵרוֹת ⊱

The blessing is recited and then the candles are lit. (When Yom Tov falls on Shabbat, first we light the candles, then we recite the blessing with the words in parentheses added.)

בָּרוּךְ אַתָּה יְיָ, אֱלֹהֵינוּ מֶלֶךְ הָעוֹלָם, אֲשֶׁר קִדְּשָׁנוּ בְּמִצְוֹתָיו וְצִוָּנוּ לְהַדְלִיק נֵר שֶׁל (שַׁבָּת וְשֶׁל) יוֹם טוֹב.

בָּרוּךְ אַתָּה יְיָ, אֱלֹהֵינוּ מֶלֶךְ הָעוֹלָם, שֶׁהֶחֱיָנוּ וְקִיְּמָנוּ וְהִגִּיעָנוּ לַזְּמַן הַזֶּה.

❧ *Eiruv Tavshilin* ☙

When Passover falls on Thursday, an *eiruv tavshilin* must be made on Wednesday for it to be permissible to cook on Yom Tov for Shabbat. The *eiruv* indicates that preparations for Shabbat have begun prior to Yom Tov. The head of the household takes some matzah and any cooked food and sets them aside until Shabbat, to be used on Shabbat. Then the following is recited:

Blessed are You, Hashem, our God, King of the universe, Who has sanctified us with His commandments and commanded us to observe the mitzvah of eiruv.

By means of this eiruv it shall be permitted to bake, cook, keep food warm, kindle flame and make all necessary preparations on Yom Tov for Shabbat for ourselves or for all Jews who live in this city.

❧ *Candle Lighting* ☙

The blessing is recited and then the candles are lit. (When Yom Tov falls on Shabbat, first we light the candles, then we recite the blessing with the words in parentheses added.)

Blessed are You, Hashem, our God, King of the universe, Who has sanctified us with His commandments and commanded us to kindle the light (of Shabbat and) of Yom Tov.

Blessed are You, Hashem, our God, King of the universe, Who has kept us alive, sustained us, and enabled us to reach this season.

The Seder Night   סדר ליל פסח

෨ סִימָנֵי הַסֵּדֶר ෩

וּרְחַץ   קַדֵּשׁ

יַחַץ   כַּרְפַּס

רָחְצָה   מַגִּיד

מַצָּה   מוֹצִיא

כּוֹרֵךְ   מָרוֹר

שֻׁלְחָן עוֹרֵךְ

בָּרֵךְ   צָפוּן

נִרְצָה   הַלֵּל

❧ *The Order of the Seder* ☙

Kadesh

Recite the Kiddush

Urchatz

Wash hands before
eating *karpas*

Karpas

Eat a vegetable dipped
in salt water

Yachatz

Break the middle matzah,
and hide the larger half
for the *Afikoman*

Maggid

Tell the story of Passover

Rachtzah

Wash hands for the meal

Motzi

Say the *HaMotzi* blessing

Matzah

Eat matzah

Maror

Eat bitter herbs

Korekh

Eat matzah and
bitter herbs together

Shulchan Orekh

Eat the festive meal

Tzafun

Eat the *Afikoman*

Barekh

Say Grace After Meals

Hallel

Sing *Hallel*

Nirtzah

Conclude the Seder

קַדֵּשׁ ୧୬

The first cup is poured and the kiddush is recited.
When the festival begins on Friday night, begin here and include all passages in parentheses.

בלחש: וַיְהִי עֶרֶב וַיְהִי בֹקֶר

יוֹם הַשִּׁשִּׁי, וַיְכֻלּוּ הַשָּׁמַיִם וְהָאָרֶץ וְכָל־צְבָאָם: וַיְכַל אֱלֹהִים בַּיּוֹם הַשְּׁבִיעִי, מְלַאכְתּוֹ אֲשֶׁר עָשָׂה, וַיִּשְׁבֹּת בַּיּוֹם הַשְּׁבִיעִי, מִכָּל־מְלַאכְתּוֹ אֲשֶׁר עָשָׂה: וַיְבָרֶךְ אֱלֹהִים אֶת־יוֹם הַשְּׁבִיעִי, וַיְקַדֵּשׁ אֹתוֹ, כִּי בוֹ שָׁבַת מִכָּל־מְלַאכְתּוֹ, אֲשֶׁר־בָּרָא אֱלֹהִים לַעֲשׂוֹת:

SHABBAT AND CREATION

The kiddush for Pesach that falls on Friday night begins with the section from *Bereishit* that describes the conclusion of the creation of the world. The division of the Torah into chapters (which originated with a thirteenth-century bishop) results in "The heaven and the earth and all their hosts were completed" becoming the opening verse of chapter two. According to a number of commentators, this division is incorrect as it creates a separation between what should be one unified subject.

Questions

1) **Explain why this division does not fit the overall structure of the *parasha*.**
2) **How does the structure of the kiddush for Shabbat support this claim?**

Suggested Answers

1) Shabbat is an integral aspect of the creation of the world. As such, it is illogical to separate the verses dealing with Shabbat from the rest of creation. The relationship between Shabbat and creation is further explored in the answer to question two in the following section, *And on the Seventh Day*.
2) The kiddush for Shabbat begins with the last verse of chapter one, "And it was evening and it was morning, the sixth day." It would have been logical to begin with verse 2:1 ("And the heaven and the earth were completed..."). This structure reflects the concept that Shabbat is integrally connected to the creation that preceded it.

๛ *Kadesh* ๛

The first cup is poured and the kiddush is recited.
When the festival begins on Friday night, begin here and include all passages in parentheses.

QUIETLY: *And it was evening and it was morning,*

the sixth day. And the heaven and the earth and all their hosts were completed.
And on the seventh day, God finished His work which He had made, and He
rested on the seventh day from all His work which He had made. And God
blessed the seventh day and made it holy, for on it He rested from all His work
which He, God, created to make.

(Bereishit 1:31, 2:1–3)

AND ON THE SEVENTH DAY

And the heaven and the earth and all their hosts were completed. And on the seventh day God finished His work which He had made, and He rested on the seventh day from all His work that He had made.

(Bereishit 2:1–3)

Genivah and the Rabbis discussed this. Genivah said: "This may be compared to a king who made a bridal chamber, which he plastered, painted, and adorned; now what did the bridal chamber lack? A bride to enter it. Similarly, what did the world still lack? Shabbat." The Rabbis said: "Imagine a king who made a signature ring: what did it lack? A signet. Similarly, what did the world lack? Shabbat."

(Bereishit Rabbah 10:9)

RASHI: R. Shimon [bar Yochai] said: "Mortal man, who does not know exactly his times or his seconds [who cannot with precise accuracy determine the point of time that marks the division between one time period and that which follows it], must add from the profane to the sacred; but the Holy One Blessed Be He who knows His times and His seconds, began it to a very hair's breadth, and it appeared as if He had completed His work on that very day." *(Bereishit 2:2)*

When the festival begins on a weekday, begin here:

סַבְרִי מָרָנָן וְרַבָּנָן וְרַבּוֹתַי:

בָּרוּךְ אַתָּה יְיָ, אֱלֹהֵינוּ מֶלֶךְ הָעוֹלָם, בּוֹרֵא פְּרִי הַגָּפֶן:

בָּרוּךְ אַתָּה יְיָ, אֱלֹהֵינוּ מֶלֶךְ הָעוֹלָם, אֲשֶׁר בָּחַר בָּנוּ מִכָּל־עָם,
וְרוֹמְמָנוּ מִכָּל־לָשׁוֹן, וְקִדְּשָׁנוּ בְּמִצְוֹתָיו, וַתִּתֶּן־לָנוּ יְיָ אֱלֹהֵינוּ
בְּאַהֲבָה (לשבת שַׁבָּתוֹת לִמְנוּחָה וּ)מוֹעֲדִים לְשִׂמְחָה, חַגִּים
וּזְמַנִּים לְשָׂשׂוֹן אֶת־יוֹם (לשבת הַשַּׁבָּת הַזֶּה וְאֶת־יוֹם) חַג
הַמַּצּוֹת הַזֶּה. זְמַן חֵרוּתֵנוּ, (לשבת בְּאַהֲבָה,) מִקְרָא קֹדֶשׁ, זֵכֶר
לִיצִיאַת מִצְרָיִם. כִּי בָנוּ בָחַרְתָּ וְאוֹתָנוּ קִדַּשְׁתָּ מִכָּל־הָעַמִּים.
(לשבת וְשַׁבָּת) וּמוֹעֲדֵי קָדְשֶׁךָ (לשבת בְּאַהֲבָה וּבְרָצוֹן) בְּשִׂמְחָה
וּבְשָׂשׂוֹן הִנְחַלְתָּנוּ: בָּרוּךְ אַתָּה יְיָ, מְקַדֵּשׁ (לשבת הַשַּׁבָּת
וְ)יִשְׂרָאֵל וְהַזְּמַנִּים:

Questions

☙1) What is the textual difficulty in *Bereishit* 2:1–3 that all of the commentators address?

☙☙2) What is the conceptual difference between Genivah's metaphor of the bride and the Rabbis' metaphor of the ring?

☙3) In what way do the views of Genivah and the Rabbis differ from that of R. Shimon Bar Yochai, as quoted by *Rashi*?

Suggested Answers

1) The first verse of chapter two seems to have an internal conflict. On the one hand, we are told that the creation of the world was completed, presumably on the sixth day. It then proceeds to say that God completed His work on the seventh day. It is thus unclear whether creation was completed on the sixth or seventh day? Furthermore, if creation was, indeed, completed on the seventh day, what was created on that day?

When the festival begins on a weekday, begin here:

With your permission, gentlemen, my masters and teachers:
Blessed are You, Lord, our God, King of the universe, who creates the fruit of
the vine.

Blessed are You, Lord our God, King of the universe, who has chosen us
from among all people, and exalted us above all tongues, and sanctified us
through His commandments. You, Lord our God, have given us with love
[Shabbatot for rest and] festivals for happiness, festivals and seasons for joy:
[this Shabbat and this] Festival of Matzot, season of our Freedom [in love],
a holy convocation in remembrance of the Exodus from Egypt. For You have
chosen us and sanctified us from all the nations, and You gave us [the Shabbat
and] Your holy festivals [with love and favor], in happiness and joy, as a
heritage. Blessed are You, God, Who sanctifies [the Shabbat and] Israel and
the festive seasons.

2) According to the bride metaphor, the six days of creation are meaningless without Shabbat. Just as the bridal chamber is purposeless without the bride, so too is the world purposeless without Shabbat. Shabbat, the spiritual realm, is the essential goal of creation.*

According to the ring metaphor, the six days of the week have meaning unto themselves, but are completed by Shabbat. This is similar to the ring, which has value as it is, but is completed by the signet.

3) According to Genivah and the Rabbis, God's act on the seventh day served in some fashion as the final step in the creation of the world. According to R. Shimon bar Yochai, there really was no aspect of creation that took place on the seventh day. The creation of the world was actually completed at the last moment of the sixth day. It only appeared to man as if something were created on the seventh day.

---

* Note: Genivah's parable of the bride is based on two other meanings of the root כ-ל-ה in the word ויכלו that is used in the biblical text relating to Shabbat. כלה can also refer to a bride and to yearnings, as in כלתה נפשי, "my soul yearns" (*Tehillim* 84:3).

If the festival falls on Saturday night, the following is recited:

בָּרוּךְ אַתָּה יְיָ, אֱלֹהֵינוּ מֶלֶךְ הָעוֹלָם, בּוֹרֵא מְאוֹרֵי הָאֵשׁ:

בָּרוּךְ אַתָּה יְיָ, אֱלֹהֵינוּ מֶלֶךְ הָעוֹלָם, הַמַּבְדִּיל בֵּין קֹדֶשׁ לְחֹל בֵּין אוֹר
לְחֹשֶׁךְ, בֵּין יִשְׂרָאֵל לָעַמִּים, בֵּין יוֹם הַשְּׁבִיעִי לְשֵׁשֶׁת יְמֵי הַמַּעֲשֶׂה. בֵּין
קְדֻשַּׁת שַׁבָּת לִקְדֻשַּׁת יוֹם טוֹב הִבְדַּלְתָּ. וְאֶת־יוֹם הַשְּׁבִיעִי מִשֵּׁשֶׁת יְמֵי
הַמַּעֲשֶׂה קִדַּשְׁתָּ. הִבְדַּלְתָּ וְקִדַּשְׁתָּ אֶת־עַמְּךָ יִשְׂרָאֵל בִּקְדֻשָּׁתֶךָ. בָּרוּךְ
אַתָּה יְיָ, הַמַּבְדִּיל בֵּין קֹדֶשׁ לְקֹדֶשׁ:

On all nights conclude here:

בָּרוּךְ אַתָּה יְיָ, אֱלֹהֵינוּ מֶלֶךְ הָעוֹלָם, שֶׁהֶחֱיָנוּ וְקִיְּמָנוּ וְהִגִּיעָנוּ
לַזְּמַן הַזֶּה:

The cup of wine should be drunk while reclining on the left side, symbolizing freedom.

SHABBAT AND THE HOLIDAYS

Shabbat shares some qualities with the holidays. In the kiddush that is recited on a regular Shabbat (that does not coincide with a holiday), we say: "For it is this day that is first among all of the days of holy gathering, a remembrance of the Exodus from Egypt."

If the festival falls on Saturday night, the following is recited:

Blessed are You, Lord our God, King of the universe, Creator of lights of fire.

Blessed are You, Lord our God, King of the universe, Who distinguishes between holiness and secular, between light and darkness, between Israel and nations, between the seventh day and the six days of activity. You have made a distinction between the holiness of Shabbat and the holiness of Chag; and You have sanctified the seventh day above the six days of labor. You distinguished and sanctified Your nation, Israel, with Your holiness. Blessed are You, God, who distinguishes between holiness (of Shabbat) and holiness (of Chag).

On all nights conclude here:

Blessed are You, Lord our God, King of the universe, who has granted us life, sustained us, and enabled us to reach this season.

The cup of wine should be drunk while reclining on the left side, symbolizing freedom.

Question
♀ **What is the meaning of this line? (for help, see *Vayikra* 23.)**

Suggested Answer
Chapter 23 of *Vayikra* begins with a statement that these are the holidays of God (מועדי ה'), and then proceeds to talk about Shabbat before mentioning the other holidays. Thus, it appears that Shabbat is the first of the holidays. Shabbat and the holidays share the aspect that they are a remembrance of the Exodus from Egypt (זכר ליציאת מצרים) but Shabbat alone is also a remembrance of the creation (זכר למעשה בראשית).

⊷ וּרְחַץ ⊶

The hands are ritually washed without a blessing.

⊷ כַּרְפַּס ⊶

All participants take a piece of *karpas* (a vegetable other than *maror*), less than the size of an olive, dip it in salt water and eat it after reciting the following blessing. You should have in mind that this blessing includes the *maror* which is eaten later on in the Seder.

בָּרוּךְ אַתָּה יְיָ, אֱלֹהֵינוּ מֶלֶךְ הָעוֹלָם, בּוֹרֵא פְּרִי הָאֲדָמָה:

⊷ יַחַץ ⊶

Break the middle matzah into two, one piece larger than the other. The larger piece is set aside to serve as *Afikoman*. The smaller piece is put back, between the two matzot.

The kiddush for Pesach that falls on Shabbat also highlights some of the differences between Shabbat and the holidays.

Questions

⚱⚱1) In the kiddush for the holidays, it states: "And you have given us…in love (באהבה) appointed times for rejoicing…," but after mentioning the specific holiday, the word "with love" (באהבה) is added a second time only if the holiday falls on Shabbat. Why? (For help, see *Gemara Shabbat* 10b, *Tosafot*: "Hanoten matana.")

2) Why does the word "Israel" (ישראל) precede the word "and the festive seasons" (והזמנים) at the conclusion of the kiddush, but when Pesach falls on Shabbat, the added word "the Shabbat" precedes "Israel" (מקדש השבת וישראל והזמנים)? (For help, see *Vayikra* 23:4 and *Rashi's* commentary.)

Suggested Answers

1) The Gemara (*Shabbat* 10b) indicates that God gave Shabbat as a gift to *Bnai Yisrael*: "I have a wonderful gift in My storehouse named Shabbat, which I wish to give to Israel. Go and inform them." The Gemara adds: "The one who gives a gift to his friend must inform him." If it is true that one who gives a gift

∞ Urchatz ∞

The hands are ritually washed without a blessing.

∞ Karpas ∞

All participants take a piece of *karpas* (a vegetable other than *maror*), less than the size of an olive, dip it in salt water and eat it after reciting the following blessing. You should have in mind that this blessing includes the *maror* which is eaten later on in the Seder.

Blessed are You, Lord our God, King of the universe, who creates the fruit of the earth.

∞ Yachatz ∞

Break the middle matzah into two, one piece larger than the other. The larger piece is set aside to serve as *Afikoman*. The smaller piece is put back, between the two matzot.

is required to inform the recipient, why are we encouraged to give charity anonymously? *Tosafot* explains that only when gifts are given out of love does the giver have to inform the recipient. From this Tosafot we can derive that Shabbat was given by God to *Bnai Yisrael* as an act of love. We therefore only add the word "באהבה" to the kiddush on Shabbat.

2) Shabbat was sanctified by God as indicated in *Bereishit* 2:3: "And God blessed the seventh day and sanctified it...." The holidays, however, are sanctified by *Bnai Yisrael* through קידוש החודש (see *Rashi*, *Shemot* 12:2), the setting of the new month, as described in *Vayikra* 23:4: "These are the feasts of the Lord, which you shall proclaim in their seasons."

RASHI: Here it is referring to קידוש החודש [the sanctification of the new month as determined by the court based on the testimony of witnesses].

R. Shimshon Raphael Hirsch learns the same concept from the fact that Shabbat is mentioned in *Vayikra* 23 before the other holidays: "Shabbat is first among the holy gatherings. It is the only one that was set and sanctified by God [and not by the court] for eternity."

Thus, the order of mentioning makes sense—"Who sanctifies the Shabbat, Israel and the holidays."

⊰ מַגִּיד ⊱

Raise the matzot and say:

הָא לַחְמָא עַנְיָא דִּי אֲכָלוּ אַבְהָתָנָא בְּאַרְעָא דְמִצְרָיִם. כָּל דִּכְפִין יֵיתֵי וְיֵכוֹל, כָּל דְּצָרִיךְ יֵיתֵי וְיִפְסַח. הָשַׁתָּא הָכָא, לְשָׁנָה הַבָּאָה בְּאַרְעָא דְיִשְׂרָאֵל. הָשַׁתָּא עַבְדֵי, לְשָׁנָה הַבָּאָה בְּנֵי חוֹרִין:

The matzot are uncovered, and the second cup is poured.

מַה נִּשְׁתַּנָּה הַלַּיְלָה הַזֶּה מִכָּל הַלֵּילוֹת? שֶׁבְּכָל הַלֵּילוֹת אָנוּ אוֹכְלִין חָמֵץ וּמַצָּה. הַלַּיְלָה הַזֶּה כֻּלּוֹ מַצָּה: שֶׁבְּכָל הַלֵּילוֹת אָנוּ אוֹכְלִין שְׁאָר יְרָקוֹת הַלַּיְלָה הַזֶּה מָרוֹר: שֶׁבְּכָל הַלֵּילוֹת אֵין אָנוּ מַטְבִּילִין אֲפִילוּ פַּעַם אֶחָת. הַלַּיְלָה הַזֶּה שְׁתֵּי פְעָמִים: שֶׁבְּכָל הַלֵּילוֹת אָנוּ אוֹכְלִין בֵּין יוֹשְׁבִין וּבֵין מְסֻבִּין. הַלַּיְלָה הַזֶּה כֻּלָּנוּ מְסֻבִּין:

The Four Questions – ארבע הקושיות

Nechama liked to refer to the four questions to demonstrate the difference between a קושיה and a שאלה. The four questions, she pointed out, are referred to as the ארבע קושיות rather than the ארבע שאלות. This is based on the way in which the questions are framed.

Each of the four questions follows the same format:

ஐ *Maggid* ଓ

Raise the matzot and say:

This is the bread of affliction *that our fathers ate in the land of Egypt. Whoever is hungry, let him come and eat; whoever is in need, let him come and celebrate the Pesach festival. This year we are here; next year may we be in the land of Israel. This year we are slaves; next year may we be free people.*

The matzot are uncovered, and the second cup is poured.

What makes this night different *from all other nights? On all other nights we eat chametz or matzah, but on this night only matzah. On all other nights we eat any kind of vegetable, but on this night we eat maror. On all nights we need not dip even once, but on this night we do so twice! On all other nights we eat sitting upright or reclining, but on this night we all recline.*

On all other nights we _____ , but tonight we _____ .

According to Nechama, this format represents a קושיה, as opposed to the simple שאלה format which would be:

Why on this night do we _____ ?

The שאלה is a simple informational question. The קושיה, on the other hand, takes note of something that deviates from the norm, reflecting a contrast or seeming contradiction to what we know, and would expect, based on previous knowledge or experience. It is thus a sharper question that requires a more specific answer. The קושיה is the fundamental pedagogic instrument of both the Pesach Seder and of biblical exegesis. Nechama's insight turns what many think of as the child's part of the Seder ritual into a sophisticated paradigm for Torah learning.

עֲבָדִים הָיִינוּ לְפַרְעֹה בְּמִצְרָיִם. וַיּוֹצִיאֵנוּ יְיָ
אֱלֹהֵינוּ מִשָּׁם, בְּיָד חֲזָקָה וּבִזְרוֹעַ
נְטוּיָה, וְאִלּוּ לֹא הוֹצִיא הַקָּדוֹשׁ בָּרוּךְ הוּא אֶת־אֲבוֹתֵינוּ
מִמִּצְרַיִם, הֲרֵי אָנוּ וּבָנֵינוּ וּבְנֵי בָנֵינוּ, מְשֻׁעְבָּדִים הָיִינוּ לְפַרְעֹה
בְּמִצְרָיִם. וַאֲפִילוּ כֻּלָּנוּ חֲכָמִים, כֻּלָּנוּ נְבוֹנִים, כֻּלָּנוּ זְקֵנִים,
כֻּלָּנוּ יוֹדְעִים אֶת־הַתּוֹרָה, מִצְוָה עָלֵינוּ לְסַפֵּר בִּיצִיאַת
מִצְרָיִם. וְכָל הַמַּרְבֶּה לְסַפֵּר בִּיצִיאַת מִצְרַיִם, הֲרֵי זֶה מְשֻׁבָּח:

RELATING THE STORY OF THE EXODUS

The Maggid section of the Haggadah is designed to fulfill the commandment of telling the story of the Exodus from Egypt (סיפור יציאת מצרים). This concept is referred to in several places in the Torah, including the following verse:

ולמען תספר באזני בנך ובן בנך את אשר התעללתי במצרים ואת אתתי אשר שמתי בם וידעתם כי אני ה' (שמות י:ב)

In order that you (sing.) may tell your child and your grandchild the things I have done in Egypt, and the signs that I have done among them, that you (pl.) may know that I am the Lord.

(Shemot 10:2)

Questions

1) Explain the change from the second person singular form (תספר) to the second person plural form (וידעתם) in this verse.

2) Why does the Haggadah use the phrase "לספר ביציאת מצרים" to describe the discussion of the Exodus at the Seder, rather than using the phrase "לספר את יציאת מצרים"?

We were slaves *to Pharaoh in Egypt, and the Lord, our God, took us out from there with a mighty hand and with an outstretched arm. If the Holy One Blessed be He had not taken our fathers out of Egypt, then we, our children and our children's children would still be enslaved to Pharaoh in Egypt. Even if all of us were wise, all of us understanding, all elders and versed in the knowledge of the Torah, we would still be obligated to discuss the Exodus from Egypt; and everyone who discusses the Exodus from Egypt at length is praiseworthy.*

Suggested Answers

1) The change in number indicates the impact of education—that by one individual telling the story to his child or grandchild, many in the end will know and understand the meaning of the Exodus from Egypt. The fact that the verb remains in the second person ("you will know"), rather than the third person ("they will know"), also reflects an important educational element—that in a true educational dialogue, the one who is apparently transmitting knowledge also learns and grows.

2) The usage of the letter ב (lit. "in" or "with") reflects a very high level of engagement in the discussion. It is similar to the phrase "וירא בסבלותם" ("and he observed their suffering") in *Shemot* 2:11. *Rashi* explains there that the phrase indicates Moshe's deep involvement in the pain of the *Bnai Yisrael* (רש"י - "השתתפות בצערי"). Similarly, it was the deep involvement of Rabbi Akiva and his colleagues in the complex discussion of the Exodus that caused them to almost miss the morning prayers as described in the next passage (היו מספרים ביציאת מצרים).

מַעֲשֶׂה בְּרַבִּי אֱלִיעֶזֶר, וְרַבִּי יְהוֹשֻׁעַ, וְרַבִּי אֶלְעָזָר
בֶּן־עֲזַרְיָה, וְרַבִּי עֲקִיבָא, וְרַבִּי טַרְפוֹן, שֶׁהָיוּ
מְסֻבִּין בִּבְנֵי־בְרַק, וְהָיוּ מְסַפְּרִים בִּיצִיאַת מִצְרַיִם, כָּל־אוֹתוֹ
הַלַּיְלָה, עַד שֶׁבָּאוּ תַלְמִידֵיהֶם וְאָמְרוּ לָהֶם: רַבּוֹתֵינוּ, הִגִּיעַ
זְמַן קְרִיאַת שְׁמַע, שֶׁל שַׁחֲרִית:

אָמַר רַבִּי אֶלְעָזָר בֶּן־עֲזַרְיָה. הֲרֵי אֲנִי כְּבֶן שִׁבְעִים שָׁנָה,
וְלֹא זָכִיתִי, שֶׁתֵּאָמֵר יְצִיאַת מִצְרַיִם בַּלֵּילוֹת. עַד
שֶׁדְּרָשָׁה בֶּן זוֹמָא. שֶׁנֶּאֱמַר: לְמַעַן תִּזְכֹּר, אֶת יוֹם צֵאתְךָ
מֵאֶרֶץ מִצְרַיִם, כֹּל יְמֵי חַיֶּיךָ. יְמֵי חַיֶּיךָ הַיָּמִים. כֹּל יְמֵי חַיֶּיךָ
הַלֵּילוֹת. וַחֲכָמִים אוֹמְרִים: יְמֵי חַיֶּיךָ הָעוֹלָם הַזֶּה. כֹּל יְמֵי
חַיֶּיךָ לְהָבִיא לִימוֹת הַמָּשִׁיחַ:

"THE TIME HAS COME TO RECITE THE MORNING SHEMA"

ליל שמרים הוא לה׳ להוציאם מארץ מצרים הוא הלילה הזה לה׳ שמרים לכל בני ישראל לדרתם. (שמות יב:מב)

It is a night of vigil to the Lord for bringing them out from the land of Egypt; this is the night for the Lord, a night of vigil for all of the Children of Israel for generations. (Shemot 12:42)

IBN EZRA: ליל שימרים הוא לה׳—The meaning is that because God watched over

them, and didn't let the destruction plague their homes, He commanded that this should be a night of "watching" for all of the Bnai Yisrael for the generations, i.e., the observance of the eating of the Pesach offering according to its regulations with matzah and bitter herbs.

There are those who explain it as similar to "the watchmen of the walls" ("שומרי החומות" – Shir Hashirim 5:7)—that they would not sleep, but would only recount the strength of God when He took them

It happened *that Rabbi Eliezer, Rabbi Yehoshua, Rabbi Elazar ben Azaryah, Rabbi Akiva and Rabbi Tarphon sat reclining [at a Seder] in Bnei Brak. They were discussing the Exodus from Egypt all that night, until their students came and told them: "Our Masters! The time has come to recite the morning Shema!"*

Rabbi Elazar ben Azaryah said: *"I am like a seventy-year-old man, yet I did not succeed in proving that the Exodus from Egypt must be mentioned at night—until Ben Zoma explained the verse (Devarim 16:3): 'In order that you may remember the day you left Egypt all the days of your life.' 'The days of your life' would mean only the days; the additional word 'all' indicates the inclusion of the nights!" The Sages, however, say that "the days of your life" would mean only the present world; the addition of "all" includes the days of Mashiach.*

out of Egypt. This explanation is supported by the statement of the disciples to their Rabbis [in the Haggadah text shown above] that "the time has come for reciting the morning *Shema.*"

Question

What is the difference between Ibn Ezra's two explanations of the phrase שימורים לכל בני ישראל לדורותם?

Suggested Answer

The first explanation interprets the word שימורים to mean "observance of mitzvot,"

a usage that is prevalent in this section of *Shemot.*

The second explanation interprets the word based on the sense of "standing watch" or "guarding over," a usage that, according to *Ibn Ezra*, parallels the connotation of the term in the first part of the verse (that God watched over and protected *Bnai Yisrael* on this night). This explanation is also reflected in the Haggadah—just as the "watchmen of the walls" stay up all night, so too did Rabbi Akiva and his colleagues stay up all night discussing the Exodus from Egypt.

בָּרוּךְ הַמָּקוֹם. בָּרוּךְ הוּא. בָּרוּךְ שֶׁנָּתַן תּוֹרָה לְעַמּוֹ יִשְׂרָאֵל. בָּרוּךְ הוּא. כְּנֶגֶד אַרְבָּעָה בָנִים דִּבְּרָה תוֹרָה. אֶחָד חָכָם, וְאֶחָד רָשָׁע, וְאֶחָד תָּם, וְאֶחָד שֶׁאֵינוֹ יוֹדֵעַ לִשְׁאוֹל:

חָכָם מַה הוּא אוֹמֵר? מָה הָעֵדֹת וְהַחֻקִּים וְהַמִּשְׁפָּטִים, אֲשֶׁר צִוָּה יְיָ אֱלֹהֵינוּ אֶתְכֶם? וְאַף אַתָּה אֱמָר־לוֹ כְּהִלְכוֹת הַפֶּסַח: אֵין מַפְטִירִין אַחַר הַפֶּסַח אֲפִיקוֹמָן:

רָשָׁע מַה הוּא אוֹמֵר? מָה הָעֲבֹדָה הַזֹּאת לָכֶם? לָכֶם וְלֹא לוֹ. וּלְפִי שֶׁהוֹצִיא אֶת־עַצְמוֹ מִן הַכְּלָל, כָּפַר בָּעִקָּר. וְאַף אַתָּה הַקְהֵה אֶת־שִׁנָּיו, וֶאֱמָר־לוֹ: בַּעֲבוּר זֶה, עָשָׂה יְיָ לִי, בְּצֵאתִי מִמִּצְרָיִם, לִי וְלֹא־לוֹ. אִלּוּ הָיָה שָׁם, לֹא הָיָה נִגְאָל:

The Four Children

The text of the Haggadah that deals with the four sons is taken directly from the *Midrash Mechilta*. The midrash is based on the following four verses in the Torah:

A. The Wicked Child – רשע
והיה כי יאמרו אליכם בניכם מה העבודה הזאת לכם, ואמרתם זבח פסח הוא לה׳....
And it will come to pass when your children will say to you, "What is the meaning of this service to you?" And you shall say, "It is a Passover offering to God...." (*Shemot* 12:26–27)

B. The Child Who Does Not Know How to Ask – שאינו יודע לשאול
והגדת לבנך ביום ההוא לאמר בעבור זה עשה ה׳ לי בצאתי ממצרים.
And you shall tell your son on that day saying, "It is because of this, that the Lord did for me when I left Egypt." (*Shemot* 13:8)

Blessed is God, blessed be He! Blessed is He who gave the Torah to His people Israel, blessed be He! Concerning four sons, the Torah speaks: One is wise, one is wicked, one is simple and one does not know how to ask.

The wise one—*what does he say? "What are the testimonies, the statutes and the laws which the Lord, our God, has commanded you?" You, in turn, shall instruct him in the laws of the Pesach offering: one may not eat dessert after the Pesach offering.*

The wicked one—*what does he say? "What is this service to you?!" He says "to you," thereby excluding himself. By excluding himself, he denies the basic principle of our faith. Therefore you should blunt his teeth and say to him: "It is because of this that the Lord did [all these miracles] for me when I left Egypt"; "for me"—but not for him! Had he been there, he would not have been redeemed!*

c. The Simple Child – תם

והיה כי ישאלך בנך מחר לאמר מה
זאת ואמרת אליו בחזק יד הוציאנו ה'
ממצרים....

And it shall be when your son asks you on the morrow saying, "What is this?" And you shall say to him, "With a strong hand, the Lord took us out of Egypt...."

(*Shemot* 13:14)

D. The Wise Child – חכם

כי ישאלך בנך מחר לאמר מה העדות
והחקים והמשפטים אשר צוה ה' אלהינו
אתכם ואמרת לבנך עבדים היינו לפרעה
במצרים ויוציאנו ה' ממצרים ביד חזקה....

When your son asks you on the morrow saying, "What are the testimonies, the statutes and the laws that the Lord our God has commanded you?" And you shall say to your son, "We were slaves to Pharaoh in Egypt and God took us out of Egypt with an outstretched arm...." (*Devarim* 6:20–21)

תָּם מַה הוּא אוֹמֵר? מַה זֹּאת? וְאָמַרְתָּ אֵלָיו: בְּחֹזֶק יָד
הוֹצִיאָנוּ יְיָ מִמִּצְרַיִם מִבֵּית עֲבָדִים:

וְשֶׁאֵינוֹ יוֹדֵעַ לִשְׁאוֹל, אַתְּ פְּתַח לוֹ. שֶׁנֶּאֱמַר: וְהִגַּדְתָּ
לְבִנְךָ, בַּיּוֹם הַהוּא לֵאמֹר: בַּעֲבוּר זֶה עָשָׂה יְיָ
לִי, בְּצֵאתִי מִמִּצְרָיִם:

FINDING THE FOUR SONS IN THE BIBLICAL TEXT

Question

One feature of rabbinic biblical exegesis is a sensitivity to a lack of parallelism in similar verses. What distinctions in the above four verses enabled the Rabbis to identify each one with a particular son?

Suggested Answer

In three cases, the child approaches the parent, but in *Shemot* 13:8, the child does not initiate the conversation. The midrash, therefore, deduces that this is a child that does not know how to ask the question.

In the three remaining verses, where the child initiates the conversation, two ask a question, but one (in *Shemot* 12:26) makes a statement (כי יאמרו אליכם בניכם). This son, the midrash concludes, is the wicked son who is not questioning, but challenging. This child's question is detailed, as is the question of the child in *Devarim* 6:20. The fact, however, that he does not refer to God strengthens the midrashic identification. Furthermore, this son is the only one to use the term עבודה to describe the ritual of Pesach. In this way he tries to equate the עבודה inherent in the Pesach service with the עבדות, the oppressive enslavement perpetrated by the Egyptians.

Of the two remaining sons who both ask a question, one (*Devarim* 6:20) asks a detailed question, and the other (*Shemot* 13:14) asks a very simple question. On this basis, the midrash identifies the first as the wise son, and the latter as the simple son.

The simple one—*what does he say? "What is this?" Tell him: "With a strong hand did the Lord take us out of Egypt, from the house of bondage."*

As for the one who does not know how to ask—*you must prompt him, as it says: "You shall tell your child on that day: 'It is because of this that the Lord did [all these miracles] for me when I left Egypt.'"*

HOW DO WE KNOW THAT THE "WICKED" SON IS TRULY WICKED?

The answer given to the wicked son seems very harsh, emphasizing in a negative way the use of the word "to you" (לכם) in his question. This response seems unjustified since the wise son also said "to you" (אתכם) in his question.* Many commentaries have tried to identify the critical distinction between the questions of the wise son and the wicked son. The following is the comment of *Akeidat Yitzchak* (R. Yitzchak Arama):

> In the Haggadah, why do the Rabbis attribute the question "What is this service to *you*" to the wicked son, and conclude that he has excluded himself from the group? Did not the wise son also ask, "which the Lord our God commanded *you?*" And the fact that the wise son uses the expression "our God" is not a complete answer, for it is possible that he accepts the existence of God, but not the validity of the mitzvot.

Questions

1) What does Arama mean when he refers to "the expression 'our God'"?

☞2) Can you resolve his difficulty in an alternative way (not using the expression "our God")? (For help, see *Yehoshua* 22:24.)

---

* Nechama noted that the original reading of the *Mechilta* actually used the term "to us" (אותנו) in the question of the wise son. This seems to be inconsistent with the reading in the Torah. R. David Tzvi Hoffman in *Beit Va'ad LeChakhamim* explains that the Torah is written as a third party describing the statement of the son. The *Mechilta* is describing the actual statement of the son and is therefore accurate in using "to us" (אותנו). This reading would further accentuate the difference between the wise and the wicked son.

3) The answer given to the wicked son in the midrash is not the same as the answer given in the Torah. Rather it is the answer given to the son who does not know how to ask. Why is this?

Suggested Answers

1) Arama is referring to the fact that the wise son included the phrase "the Lord our God" in his question, while the wicked son does not. According to Arama, this is not sufficient evidence to make the distinction between the two sons, particularly since both sons use the phrase "to you" (אתכם, לכם) in their respective questions. He claims that the son in *Devarim* 6:20 may believe in God, but not in the mitzvot.

2) The critical distinction between the wise and wicked sons must be found elsewhere. Arama suggests that the use of the phrase "when your children will say to you" rather than "when your children will ask you" indicates that this son is intent on undermining and challenging. This interpretation is supported by the

verse in *Yehoshua* 22:24 which uses similar language and expresses a clearly challenging tone: "…in time to come your children will say to our children, saying: 'What have you to do with the Lord God of Israel?'"

("...מחר יאמרו בניכם לבנינו לאמר מה לכם ולה' אלהי ישראל.")

3) Once the midrash identified the wicked son as one who is making a challenging declaration rather than posing an actual question, the serious response given in the Torah seemed inappropriate. The wicked son, in essence, is not asking a *real* question and is thus equated in the answer with the son who does not know how to ask the question. In reality, the Torah itself does not suggest an answer to the wicked son. The response is introduced by the phrase "and you shall say" which indicates a simple declarative statement. In contrast, the response to the other three sons in the Torah is addressed directly to the son, such as "and you shall say to your son," "and you shall say to him," or "and you shall tell your son."

THE ORDER OF THE CHILDREN

Question

Why does the Haggadah bring the sons in an order that is different from the order in which the corresponding verses appear in the Torah?

Suggested Answer

The midrash seems to bring the sons in order of their intellectual ability. The son with the most complex question, the

wise son, is mentioned first. Second is his counterpart, the wicked son who is also on a high intellectual level, but is not genuinely interested in any answer. After them come the sons who are on lower intellectual planes, the simple son who asks an uncomplicated question, followed by the one who cannot ask at all.

Harav Yosef Dov Soloveitchik suggested that the criteria determining the order in which the sons are brought in the midrash include their moral level and their level of activism. The sons are actually grouped in two sets of pairs. The first son is a good person who is active in pursuit of knowledge and meaning. His counterpart is actively wicked, openly challenging his parents and the tradition. The third son is also a good person, but is less active in pursuit of knowledge. His counterpart, the one who does not ask at all, is actually a wicked child who is passive, so uninterested and uninvolved that he does not even have the ability to ask the question.

According to Rav Soloveitchik, this son is not necessarily the young child who is unable to ask questions because of his cognitive level, but rather the one who is indifferent. This structure is supported by aspects of the texts of the Torah and the midrash: 1) The wicked son and the son who does not know how to ask the question are connected to each other in the midrash in that they are given the same answer. 2) The wise son and the simple son are connected in the Torah text in that they are the two that ask questions. Similarly, in the references to these two sons, the Torah uses the word מחר (tomorrow). They are the ones who are looking toward the future. This is in contrast to the verse that refers to the son who does not know how to ask the question which uses the term היום (today).

THE FOUR CHILDREN—THE PEDAGOGICAL PRINCIPLE

Midrash Tanchuma on *Shemot* 25:

"For who is there of all flesh that has heard the voice of the living God...." (*Devarim* 5:22). You heard His voice and remained alive but the nations of the world hear and die. Come and see how the voice came to Israel, each according to his ability—the elderly heard the voice according to their ability and the young according to their ability, the lads according to their ability, the children according to their ability, the babes according to their ability, the women according to their ability, and also Moshe according to his ability, as it is stated (*Shemot* 19:19): "Moshe speaks and God answers him in a voice"—in a voice that Moshe could endure. So also, "The voice of the Lord is in strength" (*Tehillim* 29:4)—it does not say in *his* strength, but in strength, which each one could endure!

Question
What specific idea emerges from both the Mechilta cited above and this *Midrash Tanchuma?*

Suggested Answer
For instruction to be effective, it must be variated so that each person receives it on his own level. The *Mechilta* is based on the pedagogical principle expressed in the *Tanchuma.*

יָכוֹל מֵרֹאשׁ חֹדֶשׁ, תַּלְמוּד לוֹמַר בַּיּוֹם הַהוּא. אִי בַּיּוֹם הַהוּא. יָכוֹל מִבְּעוֹד יוֹם. תַּלְמוּד לוֹמַר. בַּעֲבוּר זֶה. בַּעֲבוּר זֶה לֹא אָמַרְתִּי, אֶלָּא בְּשָׁעָה שֶׁיֵּשׁ מַצָּה וּמָרוֹר מֻנָּחִים לְפָנֶיךָ:

BECAUSE OF THIS...

This midrash follows the teaching that is directed toward the child who does not know how to ask the question: והגדת לבנך ביום ההוא לאמר בעבור זה עשה ה' לי בצאתי ממצרים ("And you shall tell your son on that day, saying: 'Because of this, God did for me when I went out of Egypt.'"). The midrash uses this particular verse to prove that the mitzvah of telling the story of the Exodus from Egypt must be performed on the night of the fifteenth of Nissan. The verse itself is somewhat ambiguous as reflected in the following commentaries:

RASHI: "Because of this"—that I fulfill His commandments, such as this Pesach sacrifice, Matzah and Maror.

IBN EZRA: Rabbi Marinus maintained that the expression "ba'avur zeh" must be inverted in the sense of "zeh ba'avur"—"this is because" [i.e., "this Passover ritual is because of what the Lord did for me when I went out of Egypt"]...but how can we invert the words of the living God? We

do not eat matzah because of this. Rather, He performed wonders for us until He took us out of Egypt for the purpose of observing this service, eating matzah and refraining from chametz, which are among the initial commandments that God gave to us. In other words, He only brought us out of Egypt for the purpose of serving Him, as it says, "When you [Moshe] have brought the people out of Egypt, you shall serve God upon this mountain" (Shemot 3:12), and it is stated, "Who brought you out of the land of Egypt, to be your God" (Devarim 15:41).

Questions

1) What does "this" (זה) refer to according to the three commentators (Rashi, R. Marinus, Ibn Ezra)?

2) According to each commentator, what is the meaning of "בעבור"?

3) Does R. Marinus or Ibn Ezra agree with Rashi's interpretation?

One might think that from the beginning of the month there is an obligation to discuss the Exodus. The Torah therefore says (Shemot 13:8): "On that day." "On that day," however, could be understood to mean only during the daytime; therefore the Torah specifies, "it is because of this." The expression "because of this" can only be said when matzah and maror are placed before you.

₴4) **Why does *Rashi* add "such as" in his commentary and does not simply say, "that I fulfill His commandments, the Pesach sacrifice, Matzah and Maror."**

₴5) **Why did *Ibn Ezra* add the words "which is among the initial commandments which God gave us"?**

₴6) **What is the basic difference between *Ibn Ezra* and R. Marinus in their general conception of the function of the commandments?**

₴7) **Does the midrash interpret the verse in the same way as any of these commentators, or does it offer a new interpretation?**

Suggested Answers

1) According to *Rashi* and *Ibn Ezra*—it refers to all of the commandments.

According to R. Marinus—it refers specifically to the commandments of Pesach (Matzah, Maror etc.). R. Marinus inverts the verse so that it means: "We perform the mitzvot of Pesach because of what God did for us in Egypt."

2) According to *Rashi* and *Ibn Ezra*— "for the purpose of" (God took us out of Egypt for the purpose of fulfilling the commandments.)*

According to R. Marinus—"because of" (R. Marinus inverts the verse to read: this is because of what God did for me....)

---

* This is the usual usage of the word בעבור in the Torah as demonstrated in the following verses: *Bereishit* 21:30, 27:4, 27:19, 27:31, *Shemot* 9:14, 9:16, 19:9, 20:20.

Thus, the verse would read as follows according to each of the commentators:

RASHI AND IBN EZRA—"And you will tell your children on that day saying: For the purpose of this [fulfilling all of the commandments], God took me out of Egypt."

R. MARINUS—"And you will tell your children on that day saying: 'This [the commandments relating to Pesach] is because of what God did for me when I left Egypt.'"

3) *Ibn Ezra* shares *Rashi's* view that the Exodus from Egypt took place in order that we fulfill God's commandments.

4) The use of the phrase "such as" indicates that *Rashi* is referring to the commandments in general. In his view, the word "this" refers to Pesach, Matzah and Maror as examples of all of the commandments.

5) Ibn Ezra is also referring to all of the commandments. In his view, the word "this" refers to Matzah which represents all of the commandments because it is among the first commandments.

6) The argument between R. Marinus and *Ibn Ezra* relates to the essential function of the commandments. According to R. Marinus, the commandments are a means toward the improvement of our lives and our societal organization. According to *Ibn Ezra*, our lives and societal organization are a means for the fulfillment of the commandments. The fulfillment of the commandments is an end unto itself. As such, God brought us out of Egypt only to serve Him through the fulfillment of commandments.

7) In one sense, the midrash understands the term "זה" in the same way as does R. Marinus, referring to the commandments of Pesach that are performed at the Seder. The midrash, however, does not invert the verse. The innovative interpretation of the midrash is that בעבור זה actually relates to the Seder ritual—pointing to the objects on the Seder table that represent the various mitzvot of the holiday. Only when those objects are displayed (on the night of the fifteenth of Nissan) can the commandment to tell the story be performed.

NECHAMA: ON TAXI DRIVERS, TEACHERS AND STUDENTS

Nechama was fond of recounting stories in which she learned things from unexpected sources. These stories often took place in buses or taxis. With regard to the verse "והגדת לבנך", "And you shall teach it to your child…," Nechama recounted the following conversation that she had with a taxi driver as she was grading papers in the back of the taxi:

DRIVER: You are a teacher ("*morah*"), aren't you? Once upon a time, a teacher was called a "*melamed*." What is the difference between the two?

NECHAMA: Nothing, they are the same.

DRIVER: No, there is a difference. I'll show you. Is whiskey good for you?

NECHAMA: No.

DRIVER: Do you drink whiskey?

NECHAMA: No.

DRIVER: If not, how do you know that it isn't good for you? I'll tell you how. If you sit in a bar and watch a respectable person when he begins to drink, and observe his behavior after several drinks, you understand that drinking whiskey is not good for you. That man becomes a "*melamed*." That is why the verse in *Tehillim* 119:99 that states "from all of my teachers have I learned" reads "מכל מלמדי השכלתי" and not מכל מורי השכלתי.

Nechama recounted this story to illustrate to teachers and parents the importance of children not only learning from formal instruction, but also from personal example and life experiences.

מִתְּחִלָּה עוֹבְדֵי עֲבוֹדָה זָרָה הָיוּ אֲבוֹתֵינוּ. וְעַכְשָׁו קֵרְבָנוּ הַמָּקוֹם לַעֲבוֹדָתוֹ. שֶׁנֶּאֱמַר: וַיֹּאמֶר יְהוֹשֻׁעַ אֶל־כָּל־הָעָם. כֹּה אָמַר יְיָ אֱלֹהֵי יִשְׂרָאֵל, בְּעֵבֶר הַנָּהָר יָשְׁבוּ אֲבוֹתֵיכֶם מֵעוֹלָם, תֶּרַח אֲבִי אַבְרָהָם וַאֲבִי נָחוֹר. וַיַּעַבְדוּ אֱלֹהִים אֲחֵרִים: וָאֶקַּח אֶת־אֲבִיכֶם אֶת־אַבְרָהָם מֵעֵבֶר הַנָּהָר, וָאוֹלֵךְ אוֹתוֹ בְּכָל־אֶרֶץ כְּנָעַן. וָאַרְבֶּה אֶת־זַרְעוֹ, וָאֶתֶּן לוֹ אֶת־יִצְחָק: וָאֶתֵּן לְיִצְחָק אֶת־יַעֲקֹב וְאֶת־עֵשָׂו. וָאֶתֵּן לְעֵשָׂו אֶת־הַר שֵׂעִיר, לָרֶשֶׁת אוֹתוֹ. וְיַעֲקֹב וּבָנָיו יָרְדוּ מִצְרָיִם:

IN THE BEGINNING OUR FATHERS WORSHIPED IDOLS

The Mishna (*Pesachim* 10:4) states with regard to the telling of the story of the Exodus from Egypt: "Begin with the denigration and end with praise." The Seder is to commence with the negative part of the history of *Bnai Yisrael* which preceded the redemption from Egypt. In the Gemara (*Pesachim* 116a), Rav and Shmuel disagree as to what constitutes "the disgrace." One says that it is "We were slaves to Pharaoh in Egypt," and the other claims that it is "In the beginning our fathers were idol worshipers." Both opinions are reflected in the Haggadah, with this passage representing the latter opinion. As in the Torah, the Haggadah does not describe in any detail the idolatry of our ancestors. The *Ramban* relates to this issue in his commentary to *Bereishit* 12:2:

And behold this section did not explain the whole issue. For why would God tell him [Avraham], "leave your land and I will do for you a kindness the likes of which were never seen in the world," without prefacing with the fact that Avraham was a servant of God or completely righteous, or explaining that by leaving the land and going to another land he would become closer to God?… But the Torah did not want to discuss at length the philosophies of idol worship and to explain the differences in faith between Avraham and the Chaldean people, just as it was brief about the generation of Enosh and their innovative concepts of idolatry.

Questions

1) What is the difficulty at the beginning of *parashat Lech Lecha* that the *Ramban* is trying to solve?

2) What is the difficulty that he is trying to solve in his final statement? How does

In the beginning, *our ancestors were idol worshipers; but now God has brought us close to His service, as it is said (Yehoshua 24:2): "Yehoshua said to all the people: 'Thus said the Lord, the God of Israel, "Your fathers used to live on the other side of the river—Terach, the father of Avraham and the father of Nachor, and they served other gods. And I took your father Avraham from beyond the river, and I led him throughout the whole land of Canaan. I increased his seed and gave him Yitzchak, and to Yitzchak I gave Yaakov and Eisav. To Eisav I gave Mount Seir to inherit, and Yaakov and his sons went down to Egypt."'"*

this relate to the problem mentioned above?

Suggested Answers

1) The *parasha* begins with God's command to Avraham to leave his birthplace, and His subsequent promises regarding the good fortune that he will have. It does not provide, however, a reason for Avraham's selection by God.
2) The Torah does not provide any details regarding life in Ur Kasdim during Avra-

ham's life there. The *Ramban* explains that in principle the Torah does not want to discuss the particulars of the concepts and practices of idolatry which were an abomination. This also explains why the Torah does not describe the merit of Avraham that led to his selection. His merit lies in his rejection of the world view of the Chaldean people. To elaborate upon his merit would have necessitated a discussion of the idolatry of the Chaldeans.

THE SELECTION OF AVRAHAM

According to Nechama, the selection of Avraham reflects God's attempts, which man failed to achieve, spanning over 20 generations to realize his universal plan for mankind. The implementation of the plan on a national level—through Avraham and his descendants—is predicated on the condition that *Bnai Yisrael* would ultimately transmit God's message to the

other nations. This is the meaning of the expression in *Bereishit* 12:3: ונברכו בך כל משפחות האדמה—"And through you will all of the families of the earth be blessed." This ideal is reflected in the vision of the end of days in *Tehillim* 47: "The nobles of the nations are gathered together, the people of the God of Avraham...."*

---

* See also M. Weiss, *Mikraot Kekhavanatom*, Mossad Bialik, Jerusalem, pp. 191–92.

בָּרוּךְ שׁוֹמֵר הַבְטָחָתוֹ לְיִשְׂרָאֵל. בָּרוּךְ הוּא. שֶׁהַקָּדוֹשׁ
בָּרוּךְ הוּא חָשַׁב אֶת־הַקֵּץ, לַעֲשׂוֹת כְּמָה שֶׁאָמַר
לְאַבְרָהָם אָבִינוּ בִּבְרִית בֵּין הַבְּתָרִים, שֶׁנֶּאֱמַר: וַיֹּאמֶר
לְאַבְרָם יָדֹעַ תֵּדַע כִּי־גֵר | יִהְיֶה זַרְעֲךָ בְּאֶרֶץ לֹא לָהֶם וַעֲבָדוּם
וְעִנּוּ אֹתָם אַרְבַּע מֵאוֹת שָׁנָה: וְגַם אֶת־הַגּוֹי אֲשֶׁר יַעֲבֹדוּ דָן
אָנֹכִי. וְאַחֲרֵי כֵן יֵצְאוּ, בִּרְכֻשׁ גָּדוֹל:

THE SELECTION OF BNAI YISRAEL

The same concept is evident in the selection of *Bnai Yisrael* following the Exodus from Egypt. Nechama stressed that the concept of being chosen does not imply special privilege, but rather special responsibility. The conditional nature of the selection of *Bnai Yisrael* is expressed in the following two verses from *parashat Yitro* (19:5–6):

And now, if you will obey My voice and keep My covenant, then you shall be My own treasure from among all the nations, for all the earth is Mine. And you shall be unto Me a kingdom of priests and a holy nation.

Sforno explains these verses as follows:

You shall be My own treasure from among all the nations: Even though all of mankind is dear to Me…you will nevertheless be more treasured than all of them.

And you shall be unto Me a kingdom of priests: By virtue of the fact that you will be a nation of priests, you will be more treasured than all of them—to understand and to teach all of mankind to call on the name of God.

On this issue, Nechama quoted Professor Yitzchak Heinneman: "The Torah and the prophets based their concept of chosenness specifically on universalism." *

400 YEARS OR 210 YEARS?

Ramban makes the following comment on the verse quoted in this section:
This is (מקרא מסורס) an inverted

verse, and it should therefore be read as follows: "That your descendants will be strangers in a land that is not theirs

---

* Yitzchak Heinemann, "*Bechirat Yisrael BeMikra*," Sinai, Kislev 5705, p. 18.

Blessed is He who keeps His promise to Israel, blessed be He! For the Holy One Blessed be He calculated the end [of the bondage], in order to do as He had said to our father Avraham at the "Covenant between the Pieces," as it says (Bereishit 15:13): "And He said to Avraham, 'Know for certain that your seed will be strangers in a land that is not theirs, and they [Bnai Yisrael] will serve them and they [the Egyptians] will oppress them for 400 years. But I shall also judge the nation that they shall serve, and after that they will come out with great wealth.'" (Bereishit 15:13–14)

for 400 years, and they will serve them and they will oppress them." And He did not specify the length of the servitude and the oppression.

fully by *Rashi* on this verse. Thus, the vision of the future given by God to Avraham in this verse seems to contradict what subsequently took place.

Questions

1) **What is the textual difficulty that *Ramban* is addressing?**

℣2) **How does the *Ramban's* change in the sequence of the verse solve the problem?**

℣3) **The טעמי המקרא (cantillation notes) provide an alternative solution to this difficulty. How so?**

2) *Ramban* suggests that we understand the *verse* with a different word order. The following would be his rendition: "And He said to Avraham: 'Know for certain that your descendants will be strangers in a land that is not theirs for 400 years, and they shall serve them, and they shall oppress them.'" In this version, the period of 400 years does not define the years of servitude, but rather the period of time that they will be in a land that is not theirs. According to *Rashi*, the 400 year period began with the birth of Yitzchak.

Suggested Answers

1) The phrase "400 years" comes directly after the phrase "and they shall serve them and they shall oppress them," seemingly indicating that the period of servitude will last 400 years. In fact, the servitude in Egypt lasted only 210 years, as explained

3) The טעמי המקרא (cantillation notes) provide not only the musical score of the biblical text, but also the punctuation of the verse. The musical note that divides the verse by indicating a major pause is

called "etnachta." In this case, we would have expected the etnachta in verse 13 to be on the word להם, which would indicate the following punctuation:

> And He said to Avraham: "Know for certain that your descendants will be strangers in a land that is not *theirs*, and they shall serve them and they shall oppress them for 400 years."

In actuality, however, the etnachta falls on the word אתם, indicating the following punctuation:

And He said to Avraham: "Know for certain that your descendants will be strangers in a land that is not theirs and they shall serve them and they shall oppress *them*, for 400 years."

Based on this placement of the etnachta, the phrase "400 years" defines not only the years of servitude, but the aggregate of the years of both servitude and settlement in a land that is not theirs.

TAKING THE PROPERTY OF THE EGYPTIANS

The latter part of the verse ("But I shall also judge the nation that they shall serve, and after that they will come out with great wealth") presents a moral difficulty: What was the justification for *Bnai Yisrael* to take the property of the Egyptians when they left the country? This issue was raised in the following midrash found in *Gemara Sanhedrin* 91a:

> At one time, the children of the Egyptians brought the people of Israel to Judgment before Alexander the Great. They [the Egyptians] said to him: "Behold it says [in the Torah]: 'And God made the people favorable in the eyes of the Egyptians and they lent them (וישאילום) what they required (*Shemot* 12:36)....'" [The Egyptians then turned to the Children of Israel and said:]—"Give us the silver and gold that you took from us!"

The following are some possible solutions to the problem:

RASHBAM: And each woman shall ask of her neighbor: As a complete gift.... This is the essence of the simple meaning and provides an answer to the heretics. (*Shemot* 3:22)

CHIZKUNI: Objects of silver and gold: In place of the fields, houses and objects that the Israelites were not able to take with them. (*Shemot* 11:2)

MIDRASH CHEMDAT YAMIM: And each woman shall ask of her neighbor: Why was this mitzvah commanded to the women? For when Pharaoh decreed that all the newborn sons should be cast into the river, the women of Israel bribed the servants of Pharaoh and the Egyptians with their jewelry so they would not reveal that they would cast some of their sons [into the river] and some they would leave [alive].… And God commanded that each woman should ask from her neighbor in order to restore the situation to its previous state, to return to them what they had given. And here there is no issue of fraud, but merely the returning of an object to its owner.

Questions

1) **What is the question of the heretics referred to in the *Rashbam*, to which all of the commentators are responding?**

2) **Contrast the various answers that are given to this question.**

Suggested Answers

1) The question posed by the heretics concerns the issue of *Bnai Yisrael* seem-

ingly taking the property of the Egyptians out of Egypt under false pretenses. This assumption is based on the fact that the word "שאלה" usually refers to borrowing.*

2) According to *Rashbam*, the Egyptians voluntarily gave the property to *Bnai Yisrael* as a gift. This was a result of the fact that God made them see *Bnai Yisrael* in a favorable light. The other two commentators see the taking of the property as compensation.

According to *Chizkuni*, it is compensation for property that *Bnai Yisrael* were forced to leave behind in Egypt.

According to *Midrash Chemdat Yamim*, it was compensation for money that was given as bribes to the Egyptians to save some of the Israelite children.

OBLIGATIONS TO FREED SLAVES

Two modern commentators attempted to solve the moral difficulty of this verse by comparing the following two verses:

ונתתי את חן העם הזה בעיני מצרים
והיה כי תלכון לא תלכו ריקם.
(שמות ג:כא)

And I will give this people favor in the eyes of the Egyptians, and it will come to pass that when you go out, you shall not go out empty. (*Shemot* 3:21)

וכי תשלחנו חפשי מעמך לא תשלחנו
ריקם. (דברים טו:יג)

And when you set free [a Hebrew slave], you shall not send him out empty. (*Devarim* 15:13)

BENNO JACOB: In the heart of every Israelite the Egyptians were associated with bitter memories. It would not be surprising if an Israelite would hate an Egyptian…and would think that he does not

---

* Nechama points out that in reality the question bothering the commentators is not primarily an external challenge posed by the non-Jews regarding the behavior of *Bnai Yisrael*, but an internal religious question regarding the purpose of the commandment to ask the Egyptians for their property.

The matzot are covered and the cup of wine is raised:

וְהִיא שֶׁעָמְדָה לַאֲבוֹתֵינוּ וְלָנוּ. שֶׁלֹּא אֶחָד
בִּלְבָד, עָמַד עָלֵינוּ לְכַלוֹתֵנוּ.
אֶלָּא שֶׁבְּכָל דּוֹר וָדוֹר, עוֹמְדִים עָלֵינוּ לְכַלוֹתֵנוּ. וְהַקָּדוֹשׁ
בָּרוּךְ הוּא מַצִּילֵנוּ מִיָּדָם:

The wine cup is put down and the matzot are uncovered:

צֵא וּלְמַד, מַה בִּקֵּשׁ לָבָן הָאֲרַמִּי לַעֲשׂוֹת לְיַעֲקֹב
אָבִינוּ. שֶׁפַּרְעֹה לֹא גָזַר אֶלָּא עַל
הַזְּכָרִים, וְלָבָן בִּקֵּשׁ לַעֲקֹר אֶת־הַכֹּל.

have to fulfill the commandment relating to the stranger with regard to him: "How so? Should I show love with regard to the Egyptian when I was commanded regarding the stranger: 'You shall love him as yourself.' Didn't he oppress my fathers?" But the Torah says that in the end they sent you out as friends with gifts and objects of gold and silver, as you are commanded to do with a Hebrew slave—"You shall not send him out empty-handed." (*Devarim* 15:13)

CASSUTO: The Hebrew slave already served his master according to the number of years prescribed by God. Therefore, they deserve release, and with the release

they deserve a gift…. That's what absolute justice requires. And even though there was no court in the world that was able to force Pharaoh and his aides to fulfill their obligation, the heavenly court worries about the requirements of the law.

Questions

1) For what purpose do the two commentators use verse 15:13 in *Devarim*?

2) What is the difference between the answers of the two commentators?

Suggested Answers

1) The parallelism in the two verses reflects the parallelism of the two

The matzot are covered and the cup of wine is raised:

This [promise] has sustained *our fathers and us! For not only one enemy has risen against us to destroy us, but in every generation they rise against us to destroy us; and the Holy One Blessed be He saves us from their hand.*

The wine cup is put down and the matzot are uncovered:

Go and learn *what Lavan the Aramean wanted to do to our father Yaakov. For Pharaoh had issued a decree only against the male children only, but Lavan wanted to uproot everyone.*

situations—the transition from slavery to freedom. According to each commentator, the reason for the parting gifts in each situation is the same.

2) According to Jacob, the purpose of the gift is to repair the relationship between the slave and his former master. The gift is designed to create a relationship of friendship for the future. According to Cassuto, the gift is compensation for the work done by the slave on behalf of the master during the period of enslavement. The gift fulfills the requirement of justice, correcting a wrong from the past.

THE FIRST FRUIT DECLARATION

The central section of the Maggid portion of the Haggadah consists of a study of *Devarim* 26:5–8. This text was recited by farmers who brought their first fruits (*Bikkurim*) to the Temple in Jerusalem. Several reasons have been suggested for the observance of this mitzvah and the recitation of this text:

RAMBAM, GUIDE FOR THE PERPLEXED (SEC. 3): The reading of the *Bikkurim* text fosters the quality of humility. For

שֶׁנֶּאֱמַר: אֲרַמִּי אֹבֵד אָבִי, וַיֵּרֶד מִצְרַיְמָה, וַיָּגָר שָׁם בִּמְתֵי מְעָט. וַיְהִי שָׁם לְגוֹי גָּדוֹל, עָצוּם וָרָב:

he lifts a basket (of the first fruits) on his shoulders and recognizes the kindness and goodness of God, in order to teach man that it is necessary in the service of God to recall experiences of suffering and distress in a later period of prosperity.

ABARBANEL: In order that he should subdue his passion—for the first fruits are dear to him…and he is therefore commanded to subdue his passion and not eat it, but rather he should give it to the Temple (i.e., the priests).

AKEIDAT YITZCHAK: Because the essence of accepting Divine sovereignty is that a person should recognize that all good comes from Him, and that the person's own strength and effort are not in any way responsible for his accomplishments…. For in truth the bringing of the first fruits and other offerings teaches the Lordship of God.

Questions

1) Explain the educational goals behind the various reasons given for the first fruits ceremony.

2) Which of these explanations best connects the Bikkurim ceremony to the Pesach Seder?

Suggested Answers

1) Rambam, Abarbanel and Akeidat Yitzchak all claim that the purpose of the Bikkurim ceremony is to improve the personal character of the individual. According to Abarbanel, it is to teach self-control. According to Rambam and Akeidat Yitzchak, it is to teach humility. In the formulation of Akeidat Yitzchak, it shows that all achievement does not come from human strength, but rather from God. According to Rambam's formulation, it is achieved by remembering previous experiences of suffering and distress.

2) The Rambam's explanation relates directly to the Pesach Seder. At the Seder, we recall the bitterness of the Egyptian bondage in order to better understand our freedom and its responsibilities. In a later portion of the Rambam's discussion of Bikkurim, he mentions other commandments that parallel this process including "and you shall remember that you were slaves in the land of Egypt" and "in order that you shall tell it to your children," both of which relate to the Seder.

As it is said: "The Aramean sought to destroy my father; and he went down to Egypt and sojourned there, few in number; and he became there a nation—great and mighty and numerous." (Devarim 26:5)

"THE ARAMEAN SOUGHT TO DESTROY MY FATHER"

The first three words of this verse are very difficult to understand and have generated a number of explanations:

RASHI: Lavan sought to uproot everything when he chased after Yaakov. And since he had the intention of doing so, God considers it as if he did it.

IBN EZRA: The verb "oved" (אובד) is an intransitive verb (does not take an object). If the verse were referring to Lavan, it would read "ma'avid" (מאביד) or "me'abed" (מאבד).... But it is more logical that the Arami is Yaakov, and the verse is saying that when my father was in Aram, he was poor (i.e., "my father Yaakov was a poor Aramean").

RASHBAM: My father Avraham was an Aramean, wandering and exiled from the land of Aram (i.e., "my father Avraham was a wandering Aramean.")

Questions

1) Which two of the explanations are similar, and which one is different? How so?

2) Which commentator's opinion is reflected in the Haggadah?

Suggested Answers

1) *Ibn Ezra* and *Rashbam* are similar in the explanations they provide. Although *Ibn Ezra* identifies the *Arami* as Yaakov and *Rashbam* identifies him as Avraham, they both see the verb "oved" (אובד) as an intransitive verb meaning "wandering," and the word "avi" (אבי) as the subject. *Rashi* views "oved" as a transitive verb meaning "destroyed," and the word "avi" as the object. He identifies the *Arami* as Lavan and "avi" as Yaakov.

2) *Rashi's* interpretation, taken from the midrash, is reflected in the Haggadah.

וַיֵּרֶד מִצְרַיְמָה, אָנוּס עַל פִּי הַדִּבּוּר.

AND HE WENT DOWN TO EGYPT

The identification of the Arami as Lavan raises other difficulties, as expressed by *Akeidat Yitzchak*:

All of my life I was puzzled by this verse.... For in truth, according to the simple meaning of the text, Lavan did not seek to destroy Yaakov.... And even if we assume that he intended to harm him, what is the relevance of him [Lavan] to "וירד מצרימה" ("And he went down to Egypt")? (*Devarim* 26:5)

Question
How do the interpretations of *Ibn Ezra* and *Rashbam* above resolve the difficulties posed by *Akeidat Yitzchak?*

Suggested Answer
According to *Ibn Ezra* and *Rashbam*, the text does not refer to Lavan. In their opinions, the subject is either Yaakov or Avraham, both of who went down to Egypt in their wanderings.

Let us look at *Rashi's* comment on this verse:

And he went down to Egypt: And others came upon us to destroy us, and after that Yaakov went down to Egypt.

Questions
1) What difficulty is *Rashi* addressing in the verse?

2) Why does he add the words "and others," which do not appear in the verse?

⅋⅋3) How are *Akeidat Yitzchak's* questions resolved by this *Rashi* and the previous *Rashi* on ארמי אובד אבי?

Suggested Answers
1) *Rashi* is responding to a difficulty posed by his identification of the *Arami* as Lavan who sought to destroy Yaakov: it is clear from the Torah that Lavan had nothing to do with Yaakov's descent to Egypt. If so, why does the verse imply that Yaakov went down to Egypt because of Lavan's oppression?

2) By adding the words "and others," *Rashi* indicates that the descent to Egypt was not related to Lavan. The text merely gives a concise history without a causal relationship between the events.

3) *Akeidat Yitzchak's* first question relates to the fact that nowhere in the Torah do we see that Lavan tried to destroy Yaakov.

54

"And he went down to Egypt" forced by Divine decree.

The previous *Rashi* resolves that difficulty by indicating that Lavan had the intention to destroy Yaakov, which, according to the Torah, is considered as if he actually perpetrated the action. The second question regarding the lack of relationship between Lavan and Yaakov's descent to Egypt is resolved by adding the words "and others" as indicated in answer to question 2 above.*

"COMPELLED BY DIVINE DECREE"

Questions

1) **Where do we find this Divine decree? (There are two possible answers.)**

2) **Which answer seems more accurate?**

Suggested Answers

1) In *Bereishit* 46:3–4, God says to Yaakov: "Do not fear to go down to Egypt, for I will make you into a great nation there. I will go down with you to Egypt...." This, according to *Rashbam*, was the reference of the Haggadah to the Divine decree. *Midrash Lekach Tov*, however, proposes another reference: "Compelled by the Divine decree, as He said to our father Avraham (*Bereishit* 15:13–14): 'For your descendants will be strangers in a land that is not theirs.'"

2) The reference of the midrash seems more accurate since it reflects a Divine decision that brought about the events. In the case of Yaakov, although the events are orchestrated by God, the statement is not a decree that forces Yaakov to go down to Egypt. His motivation is to be reunited with his son, and God is simply reassuring him that He will accompany him to Egypt.

---

* Gur Aryeh (*Maharal*) defends Rashi's identification of the Arami as Lavan on both grammatical and contextual grounds.

וַיָּגָר שָׁם. מְלַמֵּד שֶׁלֹּא יָרַד יַעֲקֹב אָבִינוּ לְהִשְׁתַּקֵּעַ בְּמִצְרַיִם, אֶלָּא לָגוּר שָׁם, שֶׁנֶּאֱמַר: וַיֹּאמְרוּ אֶל־פַּרְעֹה, לָגוּר בָּאָרֶץ בָּאנוּ, כִּי אֵין מִרְעֶה לַצֹּאן אֲשֶׁר לַעֲבָדֶיךָ, כִּי כָבֵד הָרָעָב בְּאֶרֶץ כְּנָעַן. וְעַתָּה, יֵשְׁבוּ־נָא עֲבָדֶיךָ בְּאֶרֶץ גֹּשֶׁן:

בִּמְתֵי מְעָט. כְּמָה שֶׁנֶּאֱמַר: בְּשִׁבְעִים נֶפֶשׁ, יָרְדוּ אֲבֹתֶיךָ מִצְרָיְמָה. וְעַתָּה, שָׂמְךָ יְיָ אֱלֹהֶיךָ, כְּכוֹכְבֵי הַשָּׁמַיִם לָרֹב.

וַיְהִי שָׁם לְגוֹי. מְלַמֵּד שֶׁהָיוּ יִשְׂרָאֵל מְצֻיָּנִים שָׁם:

גָּדוֹל עָצוּם, כְּמָה שֶׁנֶּאֱמַר: וּבְנֵי יִשְׂרָאֵל, פָּרוּ וַיִּשְׁרְצוּ, וַיִּרְבּוּ וַיַּעַצְמוּ, בִּמְאֹד מְאֹד, וַתִּמָּלֵא הָאָרֶץ אֹתָם:

וָרָב. כְּמָה שֶׁנֶּאֱמַר: רְבָבָה כְּצֶמַח הַשָּׂדֶה נְתַתִּיךְ, וַתִּרְבִּי, וַתִּגְדְּלִי, וַתָּבֹאִי בַּעֲדִי עֲדָיִים: שָׁדַיִם נָכֹנוּ, וּשְׂעָרֵךְ צִמֵּחַ, וְאַתְּ עֵרֹם וְעֶרְיָה: וָאֶעֱבֹר עָלַיִךְ וָאֶרְאֵךְ מִתְבּוֹסֶסֶת בְּדָמָיִךְ וָאֹמַר לָךְ בְּדָמַיִךְ חֲיִי וָאֹמַר לָךְ בְּדָמַיִךְ חֲיִי.

"AND NUMEROUS"

Question

☟☟Why does the Haggadah bring the verse from *Yechezkel* as a proof text for the word "numerous" rather than relying on the verse from *Shemot* to justify all three adjectives?

Suggested Answer

The word "numerous" (רַב) in our verse seems superfluous since it apparently repeats the same idea expressed in the previous expression "great" (גָדוֹל). Therefore, the midrash must find another meaning

"And he sojourned there"—*this teaches that our father Yaakov did not go down to Egypt to settle, but only to live there temporarily. As it says: "They said to Pharaoh: 'We have come to sojourn in the land, for there is no pasture for your servants' flocks because the famine is severe in the land of Canaan; and now, please, let your servants dwell in the land of Goshen.'" (Bereishit 47:4)*

"Few in number" *as it says: "Your fathers went down to Egypt with seventy persons, and now, the Lord your God, has made you as numerous as the stars of heaven." (Devarim 10:22)*

"And he became there a nation": *this teaches that Israel was distinctive there.*

"Great and mighty," *as it says: "And the children of Israel were fruitful and increased and multiplied and became very mighty, and the land became filled with them." (Shemot 1:7)*

"And numerous," *as it says: "I caused you to thrive like the plants of the field, and you increased and grew and became very beautiful, with perfect breasts and your hair grown long. But you remained naked and bare. And I passed over you and saw you downtrodden in your blood, and I said to you, 'By your blood you shall live.' And I said to you, 'By your blood shall you live'" (Yechezkel 16:6)*

for the word "numerous." The verse in *Yechezkel* adds a supernatural element to the growth of *Bnai Yisrael* in Egypt—that it was like grass which grows quickly without our effort, and increases its growth once it is cut down. The verse also sup- plies two other images that are relevant to the Haggadah:

a) **"but you were naked and bare"**— Although *Bnai Yisrael* became numerous, they were bare of mitzvot. This was a cause

וַיָּרֵעוּ אֹתָנוּ הַמִּצְרִים וַיְעַנּוּנוּ. וַיִּתְּנוּ עָלֵינוּ עֲבֹדָה
קָשָׁה:

וַיָּרֵעוּ אֹתָנוּ הַמִּצְרִים. כְּמָה שֶׁנֶּאֱמַר: הָבָה נִתְחַכְּמָה לוֹ.
פֶּן־יִרְבֶּה, וְהָיָה כִּי־תִקְרֶאנָה מִלְחָמָה, וְנוֹסַף גַּם הוּא עַל־
שֹׂנְאֵינוּ, וְנִלְחַם־בָּנוּ וְעָלָה מִן־הָאָרֶץ:

of the enslavement in Egypt and potentially a deterrent to their redemption.

b) "and I said to you: 'through your blood you shall live,' and I said to you: 'through your blood you shall live'"—This refers to the two *mitzvot* that *Bnai Yisrael* were given to fulfill in order to make themselves worthy of redemption— the blood of the Pesach sacrifice and the blood of the circumcision. (*Mechilta*)

AND THEY WERE EVIL TOWARD US

Midrash Tannaim provides an alternative text to that of the Haggadah in relation to the interpretation of the phrase "וירעו אותנו":

And they were evil toward us, as it says: "Since I came to speak to Pharaoh in Your name, he has done evil to this people (הרע לעם הזה)."

(*Shemot* 5:23)

Questions

1) How does the Haggadah interpret the expression "וירעו אותנו"?

2) How does this interpretation deviate from the simple meaning and what necessitated this deviation?

3) Can you find an answer other than that of the Haggadah to explain this unusual grammatical form?

Suggested Answers

1) The Haggadah uses the interpretation of *Abarbanel* who translates וירעו אותנו as "and they considered us evil."

2) The simple meaning of the verse would

"The Egyptians were evil toward us and they oppressed us, and they imposed hard labor upon us." (Devarim 26:6)

"The Egyptians considered us evil" as it says: "Come, let us deal cunningly with them lest they multiply and, if then when a war breaks out, they will join our enemies and fight against us, and escape from the land." (Shemot 1:10)

be "and they treated us badly." The deviation is based on the fact that the verse reads "וירעו אותנו" rather than "וירעו לנו". The sense of the first grammatical form is that they **made** us evil, rather than that they inflicted evil on us. In the proof text used by the *Midrash Tannaim*, the parallel verse employs the form "הרע לעם"—he treated the people badly. This form, however, is not really parallel to our verse.

3) An alternative understanding would be that they caused us to be evil, in the sense that the enslavement impacted negatively on our character by inculcating in us a slave mentality. This is evident from occasions when *Bnai Yisrael* tried God in the desert, such as the incident of the golden calf. Nechama herself related it to the desire of *Bnai Yisrael* to return to Egypt (*Shemot* 16:2; *Bamidbar* 14:2–4). In her words, "the dejection and humiliation ruined our character, creating in us what is called today the 'galut mentality' in that we wanted to return to Egypt, that we did not strive for freedom and independence."

Nechama was in love with the Land of Israel. Many educators invited her for trips to the Diaspora in order to conduct professional development seminars for teachers of Torah. Nechama steadfastly refused to leave Israel, even for such a noble purpose. From the time that she arrived in Israel in 1930, she never again left *Eretz Yisrael*.

וַיְעַנּוּנוּ. כְּמָה שֶׁנֶּאֱמַר: וַיָּשִׂימוּ עָלָיו שָׂרֵי מִסִּים, לְמַעַן עַנֹּתוֹ בְּסִבְלֹתָם: וַיִּבֶן עָרֵי מִסְכְּנוֹת לְפַרְעֹה, אֶת־פִּתֹם וְאֶת־רַעַמְסֵס:

"COME LET US DEAL WISELY"

RAMBAN: Pharaoh and his advisors did not see fit to kill them by the sword, for it would be treachery to kill for no reason the people who had come to the country by order of the previous king. Also, the Egyptian people would not permit the king to commit such violence, therefore he took counsel with them. Furthermore, *Bnai Yisrael* were numerous and powerful and would wage a great war. And so, he said that they should do it with wisdom so *Bnai Yisrael* would not perceive it…. Therefore, he placed upon them a tax, for it is normal for strangers in a country to pay tax to the king…and then he secretly commanded the midwives to kill the males at birth…and after that he commanded all of his people to throw the male children into the river.

Questions

1) What, according to *Ramban*, was the policy of Pharaoh toward *Bnai Yisrael*?

2) What were the stages in the implementation of this policy?

3) What is the textual difficulty that is resolved by his approach?

Suggested Answers

1) The policy of Pharaoh was to enslave *Bnai Yisrael* and kill their male children. He implemented his plan in stages so that both *Bnai Yisrael* and the Egyptians would not perceive the ultimate goal—"the final solution."

2) Pharaoh's policy was implemented in stages:

⊱ The first stage was a public relations campaign designed to inject a sense of concern about *Bnai Yisrael* in the eyes of the Egyptians.

⊱ The second stage was to impose a tax in order to emphasize the legal distinction between *Bnai Yisrael* and the Egyptian citizens.

⊱ The third stage was imposed labor which subsequently intensified.

⊱ The fourth stage was the secret killing of the male Israelite children by the midwives.

⊱ The fifth stage was the public killing of the male Israelite children.

"And they oppressed," *as it says: "They placed taskmasters over them in order to oppress them with their burdens, and they built store cities for Pharaoh, Pitom and Ramses." (Shemot 1:11)*

3) The difficulty in the verse is the unlikelihood of a powerful king of Egypt having to consult with his people in order to deal with what he perceived to be a security threat. He should have been able to simply kill *Bnai Yisrael* as he saw fit.

THEY WILL ESCAPE FROM THE LAND

RASHI: Against our will; and our Rabbis explained: It is like a person who curses himself and attributes the curse to others—as if to say "and we will go up from the land" and they will inherit it.

Questions
1) What is the difficulty in the verse?
2) Why was *Rashi* not satisfied with his first explanation, compelling him to add the midrash of the Rabbis?

Suggested Answers
1) If *Bnai Yisrael* would be part of a successful military battle against Egypt, why would they then leave the land rather than expelling the Egyptians and remaining in the land?

2) The first answer assumes that the Egyptians did not want *Bnai Yisrael* to leave Egypt. Apparently, they benefited from the presence of the Israelites in Egypt, perhaps because *Bnai Yisrael* were productive members of society. However, *Bnai Yisrael* were not slaves at this point and would, it seems, have had the right to leave Egypt if they so wished.

"AND THEY PLACED TASKMASTERS OVER THEM..."

"And they placed taskmasters over them in order to oppress them with their burdens (למען ענותו בסבלתם)."

The term "בסבלותם" also appears in *Shemot* 2:11: "And he [Moshe] went out to his brothers and saw their burdens (וירא בסבלותם)."

Questions
1) Who is the term בסבלותם referring to in the two verses?

2) How do we know that the subject of verse 1:11 is different than that of verse 2:11?

וַיִּתְּנוּ עָלֵינוּ עֲבֹדָה קָשָׁה. כְּמָה שֶׁנֶּאֱמַר: וַיַּעֲבִדוּ מִצְרַיִם אֶת־בְּנֵי יִשְׂרָאֵל בְּפָרֶךְ:

Suggested Answers

1) In verse 1:11, the term refers to the burdens of the Egyptians, while in verse 2:11 it refers to the burdens of *Bnai Yisrael*.

2) In verse 2:11, the context indicates that the term could only refer to the burdens of *Bnai Yisrael*. In verse 1:11, however, there is a grammatical inconsistency. *Bnai Yisrael* are referred to in the verse in the singular (the nation of Israel) as reflected in the verb ענותו (afflict them). The term בסבלותם (with their burdens), however, is in the plural form. Therefore, it cannot be referring to the burdens of *Bnai Yisrael*, and consequently must be referring to the burdens of the Egyptians that were placed upon *Bnai Yisrael*.

AND THEY BUILT STORE CITIES (ערי מסכנות) FOR PHARAOH

The word מסכנות (store cities) is very rarely used in the Torah. A similar word is employed when describing the bounty of the Land of Israel in *Devarim* 8:9:

A land in which you shall eat bread without scarceness (בלא מסכנת), you shall not lack anything in it.

Question

According to some commentators, the Torah uses the word מסכנת in *Devarim* to make an association to the word מסכנות in *Shemot* 1:11. What is the association?

Suggested Answer

When times are good, there is the danger of forgetting more difficult times. When we live in freedom, we tend to forget its great value. Even when we are enjoying the bounty of the Land of Israel, the Torah wants us to remember that we were slaves in Egypt by recalling the oppression that we suffered in building the store cities for Pharaoh.

PITOM AND RAMSES

RASHI: They were not previously suitable for that purpose [of being store cities], and they made them strong and fortified for the treasury.

Question

⊻ What forced *Rashi* to say that the two cities were already in existence?

"And they imposed hard labor upon us," *as it is says: "The Egyptians made the children of Israel work with rigor." (Shemot 1:13)*

Suggested Answer

The verse should have read: "And they built Pitom and Ramses as store cities for Pharaoh." The unusual order of the words in the verse indicates that the cities already existed and were turned into store cities by the Israelite slaves.

"AND THEY IMPOSED HARD LABOR UPON US"

IBN EZRA: "With rigor": He [Pharaoh] initiated many new evils against them: At first they had to do his work. When he saw that this did not reduce their rate of reproduction, he gave permission to the Egyptians and their officers to impose even more labor than was the standard for slaves. That is the meaning of בפרך (with rigor).... And when he saw that that was not effective, he called to the midwives who were the superintendents over all of the midwives and ordered them to kill all of the male children.

Questions

1) **What is the difficulty in the verse that *Ibn Ezra* is addressing?**

2) **Why did *Ibn Ezra* introduce the midwives here, before they are mentioned in the text?**

3) **Why does *Ibn Ezra* refer to the midwives as the "superintendents over the midwives"?**

4) **How does the interpretation of *Ibn Ezra* here differ from that of *Ramban* above (הבה נתחכמה לו)?**

Suggested Answers

1) The question that *Ibn Ezra* addresses is: What does this verse add to the previous verse which already described the hard labor that was imposed on *Bnai Yisrael* by the Egyptians? *Ibn Ezra* explains that the Egyptians here imposed work that was beyond the usual standard (בפרך) of slavery.

2) *Ibn Ezra*'s interpretation indicates that Pharaoh set out to impede the growth of *Bnai Yisrael* in Egypt. He is continuously searching for a method to effectively accomplish this goal. *Ibn Ezra* introduces the midwives here to emphasize that Pharaoh's original goal was not to kill the Israelite children. This was a step that he took only when his other attempts to solve the "problem" failed.

וַנִּצְעַק אֶל־יְיָ אֱלֹהֵי אֲבֹתֵינוּ, וַיִּשְׁמַע יְיָ אֶת־קֹלֵנוּ, וַיַּרְא אֶת־עָנְיֵנוּ, וְאֶת־עֲמָלֵנוּ, וְאֶת לַחֲצֵנוּ:

וַנִּצְעַק אֶל־יְיָ אֱלֹהֵי אֲבֹתֵינוּ, כְּמָה שֶׁנֶּאֱמַר: וַיְהִי בַיָּמִים הָרַבִּים הָהֵם, וַיָּמָת מֶלֶךְ מִצְרַיִם, וַיֵּאָנְחוּ בְנֵי־יִשְׂרָאֵל מִן־הָעֲבֹדָה וַיִּזְעָקוּ. וַתַּעַל שַׁוְעָתָם אֶל־הָאֱלֹהִים מִן־הָעֲבֹדָה:

3) *Ibn Ezra* refers to the two midwives whom Pharaoh consulted as "the superintendents of the midwives" because two individuals could not possibly deal with all of the births of such a large population. *Ibn Ezra*, therefore, concludes that these midwives were responsible for all of the midwives in Egypt and were instructed to inform the others of Pharaoh's order.

4) *Ibn Ezra* describes a process of oppression that was not fully planned from the beginning, but developed progressively when each step proved to be ineffective. According to Ramban, all of the stages were planned from the beginning as part of an overall strategy.

Nechama often carried on a correspondence with individuals who would send in answers to the questions in her *Gilyonot*. She once asked in her *Gilyonot* whether Pharaoh's new decrees were designed to produce better results from the labor of the slaves, or if they had another goal. She recounted that she thought that it produced better results, until a man wrote to her in detail that in no way did it produce better results. He explained that giving menial work to a professional is tantamount to asking a great surgeon to mop the floor of the operating room before the operation, and reduces productivity. Nechama wrote back and asked the man how he was so certain of this? He replied that he was an inspector of efficiency in the Department of Labor. Nechama was a strong believer in the concept: "מכל מלמדי השכלתי"—"From all my teachers have I learned." (*Tehillim* 119:99)

"And we cried out to the Lord, the God of our fathers, and the Lord heard our voice and saw our suffering, our labor and our oppression." (Devarim 26:7)

"And we cried out to the Lord, the God of our fathers," *as it is says: "And it came to pass during that long period that the king of Egypt died; and the children of Israel groaned because of the servitude, and they cried out. And their cry for help from their servitude rose up to God." (Shemot 2:23)*

AND THE KING OF EGYPT DIED

RASHI: He came down with leprosy and he slaughtered Israelite children in order to bath in their blood.

There are similarities between this interpretation and *Rashi's* comment on *Shemot* 1:8:

> And a new king arose over Egypt who knew not Yosef.

RASHI: "Rav and Shmuel—one said it was actually a new king, and one said that it was [the same king, but] new decrees."

Question
⚥ **What is the common difficulty in the two verses?**

Suggested Answer
Both verses are lacking the standard biblical formulation for the death of a king— "and X died and Y ruled in his place." There is also a common contextual difficulty. In both cases, the death of the king is followed by an unexpected consequence. In verse 1:8, it is very unusual that the new king, who would have grown up in the royal family, would not know of Yosef. And in our verse, it is very unusual that *Bnai Yisrael* would express sadness upon the death of such a wicked king. We would have expected the opposite, a sense of relief. Therefore, *Rashi* in both instances cites explanations that in fact the king did not actually die, but rather changed his policies regarding *Bnai Yisrael* and made their lives more difficult.

וַיִּשְׁמַע יְיָ אֶת־קֹלֵנוּ. כְּמָה שֶׁנֶּאֱמַר: וַיִּשְׁמַע אֱלֹהִים אֶת־נַאֲקָתָם, וַיִּזְכֹּר אֱלֹהִים אֶת־בְּרִיתוֹ, אֶת־אַבְרָהָם, אֶת־יִצְחָק, וְאֶת יַעֲקֹב:

וַיַּרְא אֶת־עָנְיֵנוּ. זוֹ פְּרִישׁוּת דֶּרֶךְ אֶרֶץ. כְּמָה שֶׁנֶּאֱמַר: וַיַּרְא אֱלֹהִים אֶת־בְּנֵי יִשְׂרָאֵל. וַיֵּדַע אֱלֹהִים:

וְאֶת־עֲמָלֵנוּ. אֵלּוּ הַבָּנִים. כְּמָה שֶׁנֶּאֱמַר: כָּל־הַבֵּן הַיִּלּוֹד הַיְאֹרָה תַּשְׁלִיכֻהוּ, וְכָל־הַבַּת תְּחַיּוּן:

RECOGNITION OF GOD

This explanation focuses on *Shemot* 2:23–25. You may notice that God's name appears five times in these verses in a repetitive fashion.

Question

What is the reason for the unusual repetition of God's name in these verses? (Hint: compare to *Bereishit* 41:25–36 and *Bamidbar* 32:20–23.)

Suggested Answer

The repetition of God's name in these verses indicates that this is a turning point with regard to the faith of *Bnai Yisrael*.

Their previous skepticism and weakened faith is replaced by a recognition of God that is reflected in their sincere prayers. The repetition of God's name in the other two cases reflects the same process in:

1) Pharaoh's recognition that God rather than Yosef is the interpreter of the dreams; and 2) the recognition by the tribes of Reuven and Gad that they must fight for the land out of commitment to God, and not just out of commitment to their brothers. In all three instances, that which was previously considered to be a human process was now recognized to be a divinely initiated plan.

"And the Lord heard our voice," *as it says: "And God heard their moaning, and God remembered His covenant with Avraham, Yitzchak and Yaakov." (Shemot 2:24)*

"And He saw our suffering," *this refers to the separation of husband and wife, as it is said: "God saw the children of Israel and God took note." (Shemot 2:25)*

"Our burden"—*these are the sons, as it is says: "Every boy that is born, you shall throw into the river and every girl you shall keep alive." (Shemot 1:22)*

OUR BURDEN

The explanation of this verse refers to Pharaoh's order to kill all of the Israelite male children at birth. This reference is also found in the following midrash (*Vayikra Rabbah* 27:11):

EISAV SAID: "Cain was foolish in that he killed his brother during the life of his father. Didn't he know that his father would continue to have children? I will not follow suit, rather 'when the day of mourning for my father approaches, I will kill my brother Yaakov.'" (*Bereishit* 27:41)

PHARAOH SAID: "Eisav was foolish. Didn't he know that his brother would have children during the lifetime of his father? I will not follow suit, rather I will kill them on the birthstool from under their moth-ers, as it says: 'Every son that is born you shall cast into the river.'" (*Shemot* 1:22)

HAMAN SAID: "Pharaoh was foolish. Didn't he know that the girls would marry other men and have children? I will not follow suit, rather I plan 'to destroy, to kill and to annihilate all of *Bnai Yisrael*, both young and old, little children and women, on one day.'" (*Esther* 3:13)

GOG AND MAGOG in the time to come will say the same thing: "The previous ones who busied themselves with designs against Israel were foolish in that they did not realize that they [Israel] had a protector in heaven. I will not follow suit, rather I will first engage their protector and afterwards I will engage them."

וְאֶת לַחֲצֵנוּ. זֶה הַדְּחַק. כְּמָה שֶׁנֶּאֱמַר: וְגַם-רָאִיתִי אֶת-
הַלַּחַץ, אֲשֶׁר מִצְרַיִם לֹחֲצִים אֹתָם:

Questions

1) **What is the intention of the midrash in comparing Eisav, Pharaoh and Haman?**

2) **What is the difference between Eisav, Pharaoh, and Haman on the one hand, and Gog and Magog on the other?**

Suggested Answers

1) This midrash demonstrates the historical progression of cruelty and sophistication among the enemies of *Bnai Yisrael*. According to the midrash, the intention of all three of these protagonists was not simply to destroy one particular individual, but to prevent these individuals from bearing future descendants. They differed, however, in their methodology, each adopting a progressively harsher approach in order to destroy *Bnai Yisrael*. Thus, Pharaoh's order to kill the male children was not designed just to prevent a leader from arising, but rather to put an end to the continuity of *Bnai Yisrael*.

2) Eisav, Pharaoh and Haman all believed that they could annihilate *Bnai Yisrael* through physical means. Gog and Magog will understand that the strength of *Bnai Yisrael* lies in their faith. Therefore, they will first try to undermine the ideology before engaging in a physical attack.

OUR OPPRESSION

The word לחץ and its derivatives appear infrequently in the Torah. After its use to describe the oppression of *Bnai Yisrael* in Egypt, it is not used again until *parashat Mishpatim* in the following two contexts:

וגר לא תונה ולא תלחצנו כי גרים הייתם
בארץ מצרים. (שמות כב:כ)

You shall not afflict or oppress the stranger, because you were strangers in the land of Egypt. (*Shemot* 22:20)

וגר לא תלחץ ואתם ידעתם את נפש
הגר כי גרים הייתם בארץ מצרים. (שמות
כג:ט)

And you shall not oppress the stranger, for you know the soul of the stranger since you were strangers in the land of Egypt. (*Shemot* 23:9)

RASHI: If you oppress him, he can oppress you, and say: "You are also descendants of strangers."

"And our oppression"—*this refers to the pressure, as it is says: "I have seen the oppression with which the Egyptians are oppressing them." (Shemot 3:9)*

RAMBAN: You will not afflict and oppress the stranger and think that there is nobody to save him from your hand, because you know that you were strangers in Egypt, and I saw the oppression with which the Egyptians oppressed you and took vengeance.

SEFER HACHINUCH: By reminding us of the great anguish in this status, and how we ourselves already experienced it, and God in His great mercy and kindness took us out, our mercy will be aroused for any person in that situation.

Question

What is the difference between the commentators in their explanation of the reason that we are forbidden to oppress the stranger?

Suggested Answer

Our enslavement in Egypt, as it was revealed to Avraham, was part of a Divine plan with a particular purpose. All three commentators indicate that our great suffering in Egypt was designed to have an impact on our moral character.

According to *Rashi*, it created an historical precedent that would prevent us from becoming haughty. According to Ramban, it demonstrated that God is the champion of the oppressed. And according to the *Sefer Hachinuch*, it demonstrated God's mercy as a model for us to emulate.

Our reenactment of these events at the Pesach Seder is partially designed to strengthen our sensitivities to the plight of the stranger in our midst.

In 1991, Israel executed "Operation Solomon" in which 14,000 Ethiopians were secretly brought to Israel in one weekend. In the weeks following this outstanding accomplishment, Nechama referred to it many times with a sense of wonder. She never mentioned the logistical aspects of the operation. Rather, she would say: "Fourteen thousand strangers were brought to Israel in one weekend, and every one of them had a bed in which to sleep!" Nechama was in awe of the care given to these needy refugees. She considered this a unique sociological phenomenon that could only be explained by the inherent Jewish sensitivity to those who are oppressed.

וַיּוֹצִאֵנוּ יְיָ מִמִּצְרַיִם, בְּיָד חֲזָקָה, וּבִזְרֹעַ נְטוּיָה, וּבְמֹרָא גָדוֹל וּבְאֹתוֹת וּבְמֹפְתִים:

וַיּוֹצִאֵנוּ יְיָ מִמִּצְרַיִם. לֹא עַל-יְדֵי מַלְאָךְ, וְלֹא עַל-יְדֵי שָׂרָף. וְלֹא עַל-יְדֵי שָׁלִיחַ. אֶלָּא הַקָּדוֹשׁ בָּרוּךְ הוּא בִּכְבוֹדוֹ וּבְעַצְמוֹ. שֶׁנֶּאֱמַר: וְעָבַרְתִּי בְאֶרֶץ מִצְרַיִם בַּלַּיְלָה הַזֶּה, וְהִכֵּיתִי כָל-בְּכוֹר בְּאֶרֶץ מִצְרַיִם, מֵאָדָם וְעַד בְּהֵמָה, וּבְכָל-אֱלֹהֵי מִצְרַיִם אֶעֱשֶׂה שְׁפָטִים אֲנִי יְיָ:

וְעָבַרְתִּי בְאֶרֶץ-מִצְרַיִם בַּלַּיְלָה הַזֶּה, אֲנִי וְלֹא מַלְאָךְ. וְהִכֵּיתִי כָל בְּכוֹר בְּאֶרֶץ-מִצְרַיִם. אֲנִי וְלֹא שָׂרָף. וּבְכָל-אֱלֹהֵי מִצְרַיִם אֶעֱשֶׂה שְׁפָטִים, אֲנִי וְלֹא הַשָּׁלִיחַ. אֲנִי יְיָ. אֲנִי הוּא וְלֹא אַחֵר:

AT MIDNIGHT

There is some confusion in the Torah regarding the actual time of the tenth plague, the killing of the firstborn children. When the Torah describes the event (*Shemot* 12:29), it states that the plague took place at midnight (בחצי הלילה). When Moshe warned Pharaoh (*Shemot* 11:4), however, he said that God had informed him that the plague would take place around midnight (כחצות הלילה). *Rashi* explains that חצות הלילה could refer to the middle portion of the night, and not necessarily midnight. He also brings, however, the following midrash:

Moshe said כחצות which sounds like "around midnight" which might be before or after, and did not say

"And the Lord took us out of Egypt with a strong hand and an outstretched arm, and with great awe, and with signs and wonders." (Devarim 26:8)

"The Lord took us out of Egypt"—*not through an angel, not through a seraph and not through a messenger. The Holy One Blessed be He did it in His glory by Himself. As it says: "In that night I will pass through the land of Egypt, and I will smite every firstborn in the land of Egypt, from man to beast, and I will carry out judgments against all the gods of Egypt, I am the Lord." (Shemot 12:12)*

"I will pass through the land of Egypt," I and not an angel—"And I will smite every firstborn in the land of Egypt"—I and not a seraph—"And I will carry out judgments against all the gods of Egypt"—I and not a messenger—"I am the Lord"—it is I and no other.

"at midnight" (בחצות) lest Pharaoh's astrologers be mistaken and claim that Moshe is a liar. But God who knows exact times said "at midnight" (בחצות).
(*Berachot* 4a)

Question

℣ The *Imrei Shefer* asks a question on the midrash that *Rashi* quotes: "If the astrologers would make a mistake and consider Moshe a liar, why would Moshe be concerned since he has the authority of God's word?" How might you answer his question?

Suggested Answer

It really was of no concern to Moshe what the Egyptians thought of him, but his credibility as a messenger of God was important since a primary goal of the plagues was to foster a recognition of God among the Egyptians. (For a more complete discussion of the purpose of the plagues, see the section on the ten plagues.)

בְּיָד חֲזָקָה. זוֹ הַדֶּבֶר. כְּמָה שֶׁנֶּאֱמַר: הִנֵּה יַד־יְיָ הוֹיָה, בְּמִקְנְךָ אֲשֶׁר בַּשָּׂדֶה, בַּסּוּסִים בַּחֲמֹרִים בַּגְּמַלִּים, בַּבָּקָר וּבַצֹּאן, דֶּבֶר כָּבֵד מְאֹד:

וּבִזְרֹעַ נְטוּיָה. זוֹ הַחֶרֶב. כְּמָה שֶׁנֶּאֱמַר: וְחַרְבּוֹ שְׁלוּפָה בְּיָדוֹ, נְטוּיָה עַל־יְרוּשָׁלָיִם:

וּבְמוֹרָא גָדוֹל. זֶה גִּלּוּי שְׁכִינָה. כְּמָה שֶׁנֶּאֱמַר: אוֹ הֲנִסָּה אֱלֹהִים, לָבוֹא לָקַחַת לוֹ גוֹי מִקֶּרֶב גּוֹי, בְּמַסֹּת בְּאֹתֹת וּבְמוֹפְתִים וּבְמִלְחָמָה, וּבְיָד חֲזָקָה וּבִזְרוֹעַ נְטוּיָה, וּבְמוֹרָאִים גְּדֹלִים. כְּכֹל אֲשֶׁר־עָשָׂה לָכֶם יְיָ אֱלֹהֵיכֶם בְּמִצְרַיִם, לְעֵינֶיךָ:

"HAS GOD EVER TRIED TO TAKE UNTO HIMSELF A NATION FROM THE MIDST OF ANOTHER NATION?"

The Haggadah cites *Devarim* 4:34 (הנסה אלהים לבוא לקחת גוי מקרב גוי) as the proof text for the phrase, "And with great awe." The commentaries on this verse can be divided into two categories:

Category one

RASHI: הנסה אלוהים: Did any god do miracles to come and take for himself a nation from within another nation?

SHADAL: הנסה אלוהים: There is no doubt that it is a profane usage of the term [that the term אלוהים refers to pagan gods], as in *Rashi*'s opinion.

Category two

IBN EZRA: הנסה אלוהים: There are those who say that it is a profane usage of the term—Heaven forbid!

הנסה: The Torah uses human terminology so the reader (lit. listener) will understand.

RAMBAN: Because He did for you what He did not do for any other nation.

"With a mighty hand"—*this refers to the dever (pestilence) as it says: "The hand of the Lord will strike your livestock which are in the field—the horses, the donkeys, the camels, the oxen and the sheep—with a very severe pestilence." (Shemot 9:3)*

"And with an outstretched arm"—*this refers to the sword, as it says: "His sword was drawn in His hand, stretched out over Jerusalem." (Divrei Hayamim 21:16)*

"And with great awe"—*this refers to the revelation of the Divine Presence, as it says: "Has God ever tried to take unto Himself a nation from the midst of another nation, with trials, signs and wonders, with war, with a mighty hand and an outstretched arm, and with awesome revelations, like all that the Lord your God did for you in Egypt before your eyes?" (Devarim 4:34)*

Questions

1) **What is the basis for the two approaches of the commentaries to this verse?**

2) **Why does *Rashi* interpret the word "נסה" as relating to miracles rather than to its usual meaning?**

Suggested Answers

1) Each opinion is based on the emphasis that they place on the concluding phrase of the verse: "like all that the Lord your God did for you in Egypt before your eyes?" *Rashi* and *Shadal* place emphasis on the words "the Lord **your** God," as opposed to the pagan gods referred to at the beginning of the verse who are unable to do what God was able to do. *Ibn Ezra* and *Ramban* place emphasis on the word **"for you,"** meaning that God never took any other nation out as He did with you.

2) According to *Rashi*, the verse is comparing the inability of the gods to perform an act that God accomplished. He therefore interprets the word נסה as relating to miracles because it would be inappropriate to imply that God attempted to take *Bnai Yisrael* out from under the Egyptians. He did not **attempt** to take them out; He took them out in a miraculous fashion.

וּבְאֹתוֹת. זֶה הַמַּטֶּה, כְּמָה שֶׁנֶּאֱמַר: וְאֶת הַמַּטֶּה הַזֶּה תִּקַּח
בְּיָדֶךָ. אֲשֶׁר תַּעֲשֶׂה־בּוֹ אֶת־הָאֹתֹת:

וּבְמֹפְתִים. זֶה הַדָּם. כְּמָה שֶׁנֶּאֱמַר: וְנָתַתִּי מוֹפְתִים, בַּשָּׁמַיִם
וּבָאָרֶץ:

Remove one drop of wine for each of the 3 calamities:

דָּם. וָאֵשׁ. וְתִימְרוֹת עָשָׁן:

דָּבָר אַחֵר. בְּיָד חֲזָקָה שְׁתַּיִם. וּבִזְרֹעַ נְטוּיָה שְׁתַּיִם. וּבְמוֹרָא
גָּדוֹל שְׁתַּיִם. וּבְאֹתוֹת שְׁתַּיִם. וּבְמֹפְתִים שְׁתַּיִם:

THE STAFF

The staff was used in the performance of signs in Egypt and at the sea. According to the midrash, its function changed in the process:

Lift up (הרם) your staff and stretch out your hand over the sea and divide it.
(*Shemot* 11:16)

The Egyptians said: "Moshe could not do anything without the staff with which he smote the river and brought all of the plagues." When Israel came to the sea, God said to Moshe: "Cast aside your staff so that they not say

that you could not split the sea without the staff." As it says: "lift up your staff."
(*Shemot Rabbah* 21:9)

Questions
1) How does the midrash interpret the word "lift up" (הרם)?

2) What compelled the midrash to interpret it in this way?

Suggested Answers
1) The midrash translates the word הרם as "throw" rather than "lift."

"And with signs"—*this refers to the staff, as it says: "Take into your hand this staff with which you shall perform the signs." (Shemot 4:17)*

"And with wonders"—*this refers to the blood, as it says: "And I shall show wonders in the heavens and on the earth." (Yoel 3:3)*

Remove one drop of wine for each of the 3 calamities:

Blood, fire and columns of smoke.

Another interpretation of the preceding verse: With a mighty hand—two plagues. And with an outstretched arm—two. And with great awe—two. And with signs—two. And with wonders—two.

2) This interpretation is based on the fact that God did not tell Moshe to "lift up the staff and stretch it over the sea," but rather "lift up the staff and stretch your **hand** over the sea." It seems from this that the staff was cast aside and that Moshe only used his hand in parting the sea. According to the midrash, this was to wean the people of their dependency on the staff as an integral element in bringing signs and wonders.

PAIRS OF PLAGUES

This section records an additional midrashic interpretation of *Devarim* 26:8 which relates the verse to the ten plagues. The number 10 is divisible only by 2 and 5. Unlike the ten commandments which are given in two groups of five, the ten plagues are never presented in groups of five. We will soon encounter a unique grouping of the plagues into three sets presented by Rabbi Yehuda later in the Haggadah. The above midrash suggests that the plagues might be viewed as five pairs of plagues (i.e., blood—frogs, lice—wild beasts, etc.).

אֵלּוּ עֶשֶׂר מַכּוֹת שֶׁהֵבִיא הַקָּדוֹשׁ בָּרוּךְ הוּא עַל־הַמִּצְרִים
בְּמִצְרַיִם, וְאֵלּוּ הֵן:

As each of the plagues is mentioned, a drop of wine is removed from the cup.

דָּם. צְפַרְדֵּעַ. כִּנִּים. עָרוֹב. דֶּבֶר. שְׁחִין. בָּרָד. אַרְבֶּה.
חֹשֶׁךְ. מַכַּת בְּכוֹרוֹת:

Question

℣ **What might be the connection between the plagues in each grouping?**

Suggested Answer

Nechama suggested the following connections between the plagues in each pair:

1) **Blood—Frogs:** Both are related to the Nile River.

2) **Lice—Wild Beasts:** Both are swarms of living creatures.*

3) **Pestilence—Boils:** Similar diseases, one affecting animals and one affecting man.

4) **Hail—Locusts:** Two sources of damage to crops.

5) **Darkness—Killing of the Firstborn:** two types of darkness.

---

* The most commonly accepted meaning of עָרוֹב is a mixture of wild beasts. Nechama points out that there is another opinion that the word refers to a swarm of insects. In that case, the connection between the two plagues would be even stronger.

These are the Ten Plagues which the Holy One Blessed be He brought upon the Egyptians in Egypt, and they are as follows:

As each of the plagues is mentioned, a drop of wine is removed from the cup.

Blood. Frogs. Lice. Wild Beasts. Pestilence. Boils. Hail. Locusts. Darkness. Slaying of the Firstborn.

The Ten Plagues

THE PURPOSE OF THE PLAGUES

In this section, we will deal with the purpose of the plagues. We will focus primarily on the plague of blood, but some questions may draw on other sections of *parshiyot Va'era* and *Bo*. In particular, you may find the following sections of *Shemot* relevant and helpful:

General information—5:1–2, 7:3–5; Blood—7:14–17; Frogs—7:26–27, 8:4–6; Lice—8:12, 15; Wild Animals—8:16–18; Pestilence—9:1–3; Boils—9:8–9; Hail—9:13–20, 27; Locusts—10:1–4; Darkness—10:21; Slaying of the Firstborn—11:4–6.

The following are several explanations relating to the plague of blood:

RASHI (7:19): Since there is no rainfall in Egypt, but the Nile overflows and waters the land and the Egyptians worship the Nile; He therefore plagued first their god and then them.

MISHNAT R. ELIEZER: Why did He bring upon them the plague of blood? Because they threw the children of the Israelites into the river.... Therefore, He punished them through the waters of the Nile.

MIDRASH LEKACH TOV: Because they spilled the blood of the Israelites like water, their rivers turned to blood and they could not drink the water.

Questions

1) What is the difference between the explanation of *Rashi* and the two midrashim that follow?

☙2) Where else does *Rashi* express a similar view about the purpose of the plagues?

3) What references in the biblical text support *Rashi*'s view?

☙4) Where else in the story of Moshe's confrontation with Pharaoh do we find a mockery of the gods of Egypt?

5) The first part of *Rashi*'s commentary, "since there is no rainfall in Egypt, but the Nile overflows and waters the land and the Egyptians worship the Nile," does not appear in the midrash from which *Rashi* took his commentary on this verse. Why does *Rashi* add this phrase?

Suggested Answers

1) According to *Rashi* (based on *Midrash Rabbah*), the plagues served an educational purpose—for the Egyptians (and *Bnai Yisrael*) to recognize God. According to the other two midrashim, the plagues were a punishment for the Egyptians

based on the concept of "measure for measure."

2) *Rashi* emphasizes the educational nature of the plagues in his comment on *Shemot* 7:3 which introduces the concept of the plagues: "…so that I might increase My signs against him so that you will recognize My power; and so God brings punishment upon the idol-worshiping nations so Israel will hear and see…."

3) *Rashi* utilizes the midrash from *Shemot Rabbah* in his commentary because it best fits into the context. The verse in which God introduces the plague of blood states: "by this you will know that I am God…." (*Shemot* 7:17). Similar expressions appear throughout the section dealing with the ten plagues, such as 7:5, 8:6, 8:18, 9:14, 9:29, 10:2, 11:7, 14:4 and 14:18.

4) When Moshe threw down his staff before Pharaoh, it turned into a crocodile (and not into a snake as it had done earlier), because the crocodile was worshiped in Egypt.

5) *Rashi* added this phrase to explain why the Egyptians worshiped the Nile. It is a basic explanation of paganism, which deifies natural forces.

THE HARDENING OF PHARAOH'S HEART

And I will harden Pharaoh's heart and multiply my signs and wonders in the land of Egypt.

(*Shemot* 7:3)

MIDRASH RABBAH: "For I have hardened his heart" (*Shemot* 10:1): Rabbi Yochanan said: "This gives an opening to the heretics to say that he did not have the opportunity to repent".... *Resh Lakish* replied: "Let the mouths of the heretics be closed, for it states in *Tehillim* 3:34: 'He scorns the scorners.' God warns a person several times, and if he does not repent, He closes his heart to repentance in order to punish him for his sin. So it was with Pharaoh the evil one. God sent him the message five times and he did not pay attention. Therefore God said to him: 'You were stubborn and hardened your heart. Now I will add impurity to your impurity by hardening your heart.'"

SFORNO: There is no doubt that without the hardening of his heart, Pharaoh would have sent Israel out, not out of repentance and submission to God in recognition of His greatness and goodness, but rather because of his inability to withstand the suffering of the plagues. This would not be repentance at all. And God said: "I will harden Pharaoh's heart that he will have the strength to bear the plagues and will not send them out of fear...."

Questions

1) Explain the difficulty of Rabbi Yochanan.

2) How does *Resh Lakish* resolve the difficulty?

3) Prove from the Torah the assertion of *Resh Lakish* that God gave Pharaoh five chances before he hardened Pharaoh's heart.

4) **How does *Sforno*'s interpretation differ from that of *Resh Lakish*?**

Suggested Answers

1) It seems that Pharaoh did not have free will in deciding whether to release *Bnai Yisrael* since God hardened his heart. If this is the case, how can he be held responsible?

2) *Resh Lakish* replies that Pharaoh indeed had free will during the first five plagues and chose not to respond positively. As a punishment, he lost his free will in the latter five plagues and suffered the consequences of those plagues as well.

3) If we pay attention to the wording of the reaction of Pharaoh after each of the first five plagues (*Shemot* 7:22, 8:11, 8:15, 8:28, and 9:7), we note that it states that Pharaoh hardened his own heart or that Pharaoh's heart hardened. Only after the fifth plague does the Torah indicate that God hardened Pharaoh's heart.

4) *Sforno* does not see the hardening of Pharaoh's heart as a deterrent to his exercise of free will, but rather as a vehicle to **ensure** his free will. The hardening of Pharaoh's heart meant that God gave him the courage and resolve not to capitulate as a result of fear of the pain inflicted by the plagues. This kept open the gate of true repentance to Pharaoh.

רַבִּי יְהוּדָה הָיָה נוֹתֵן בָּהֶם סִמָּנִים:

Remove 3 drops of wine for each acronym:

דְּצַ"ךְ עֲדַ"שׁ בְּאַחַ"ב:

RABBI YEHUDA'S ACRONYM

Rabbi Yehuda's acronym is not just a nemonic device, but also a thematic grouping of the plagues that relates, as well, to the purpose of the plagues.

Questions

꠸1) **Explain what unites the plagues in each of the three groups.**

꠸2) **What is the recurring theme common to the first plague in each group, to the second plague in each group, and to the third plague in each group?**

Suggested Answers

1) According to *Abarbanel*, Pharaoh's response to Moshe in *Shemot* 5:2 contains within it three theological challenges:

And Pharaoh said: "Who is God that I should obey His voice to let Israel go?; I know not God, nor will I let Israel go."

"I know not God"—questions the existence of God

"Who is God?"—questions that God is involved in supervising human events

"That I should obey him"—questions God's power and ability to change the course of nature

Abarbanel claims that each group of plagues comes to refute one of Pharaoh's challenges:

Rabbi Yehuda abbreviated them by their initials:

Remove 3 drops of wine for each acronym:

DeTzaKh

blood, frogs, lice

ADaSh

wild beasts, pestilence, boils

BeAChaV

hail, locusts, darkness, slaying of the firstborn.

The first group (דצ״ך) comes to prove the existence of God. In the first plague, God states: "In order that you shall know that I am God."

The second group (עד״ש) comes to demonstrate God's role in human events. In the fourth plague (the first plague in this group), God states: "In order that you shall know that I am God in the midst of the land."

The third group (באח״ב) comes to demonstrate God's mastery over nature. In the seventh plague (the first plague in this group), God states: "In order that you shall know that there is none like Me in all of the land."

2) *Abarbanel* demonstrates the following structure of the plagues:

First plague in each group—Moshe meets Pharaoh in the morning outside of the palace (e.g. לך אל פרעה בבקר —הנה יוצא המימה ונצבת לקראתו—go to Pharaoh in the morning as he goes out to the water and stand before him).

Second plague in each group—Moshe comes to the palace to see Pharaoh (e.g. בא אל פרעה ואמרת אליו—come to Pharaoh and say to him).

Third plague in each group—Moshe performs the plague without meeting with Pharaoh first. For the first two plagues there is a warning, but for the third plague there is no warning.

רַבִּי יוֹסֵי הַגְּלִילִי אוֹמֵר: מִנַּיִן אַתָּה אוֹמֵר, שֶׁלָּקוּ הַמִּצְרִים בְּמִצְרַיִם עֶשֶׂר מַכּוֹת, וְעַל הַיָּם, לָקוּ חֲמִשִּׁים מַכּוֹת? בְּמִצְרַיִם מָה הוּא אוֹמֵר: וַיֹּאמְרוּ הַחַרְטֻמִּם אֶל־פַּרְעֹה, אֶצְבַּע אֱלֹהִים הוּא. וְעַל הַיָּם מָה הוּא אוֹמֵר? וַיַּרְא יִשְׂרָאֵל אֶת־הַיָּד הַגְּדֹלָה, אֲשֶׁר עָשָׂה יְיָ בְּמִצְרַיִם, וַיִּירְאוּ הָעָם אֶת־יְיָ. וַיַּאֲמִינוּ בַּיְיָ, וּבְמֹשֶׁה עַבְדּוֹ: כַּמָּה לָקוּ בְאֶצְבַּע, עֶשֶׂר מַכּוֹת: אֱמוֹר מֵעַתָּה, בְּמִצְרַיִם לָקוּ עֶשֶׂר מַכּוֹת, וְעַל־הַיָּם, לָקוּ חֲמִשִּׁים מַכּוֹת:

רַבִּי אֱלִיעֶזֶר אוֹמֵר: מִנַּיִן שֶׁכָּל־מַכָּה וּמַכָּה, שֶׁהֵבִיא הַקָּדוֹשׁ בָּרוּךְ הוּא עַל הַמִּצְרִים בְּמִצְרַיִם, הָיְתָה שֶׁל אַרְבַּע מַכּוֹת? שֶׁנֶּאֱמַר: יְשַׁלַּח־בָּם חֲרוֹן אַפּוֹ, עֶבְרָה וָזַעַם וְצָרָה. מִשְׁלַחַת מַלְאֲכֵי רָעִים: עֶבְרָה אַחַת. וָזַעַם שְׁתַּיִם. וְצָרָה שָׁלֹשׁ. מִשְׁלַחַת מַלְאֲכֵי רָעִים אַרְבַּע: אֱמוֹר מֵעַתָּה, בְּמִצְרַיִם לָקוּ אַרְבָּעִים מַכּוֹת, וְעַל הַיָּם לָקוּ מָאתַיִם מַכּוֹת:

THE FINGER OF GOD

In this section, Rabbi Yossi the Galilean, Rabbi Eliezer and Rabbi Akiva posit that the Egyptians suffered from five times as many plagues at the sea than they did in Egypt itself. Their comments are based on a juxtaposition of the following two verses:

Following the plague of lice: "And the sorcerers said to Pharaoh: 'It is the finger of the Lord (אלהים)'" (*Shemot* 8:15).

At the sea: "And Israel saw the great hand which God ('ה) laid upon the Egyptians...." (*Shemot* 14:31)

Rabbi Yossi the Galilean said: *How do you know that the Egyptians were struck by ten plagues in Egypt, and then were struck by fifty plagues at the sea? About the plagues in Egypt, what does it says? "The sorcerers said to Pharaoh, 'It is the finger of the Lord'" (Shemot 8:15). But of the events at sea, it says, "Israel saw the great hand that the Lord laid against Egypt; and the people feared the Lord, and they believed in the Lord and in His servant Moshe" (Shemot 14:31). How many plagues did the Egyptian receive from one finger? Ten. From here we can conclude that if they suffered ten plagues in Egypt, they suffered fifty at the sea.*

Rabbi Eliezer said: *How do we know that each individual plague which the Holy One Blessed be He brought upon the Egyptians in Egypt consisted of four plagues? For it says (Tehillim 78:49): "He sent upon his fierce anger: wrath, fury and trouble, and a team of hostile angels." Wrath is one; fury is two; trouble is three and a team of hostile angels is four. Thus from here we can conclude that in Egypt they were struck by forty plagues, and at the sea they were struck by 200 plagues.*

The statement of the sorcerers is explained by several commentators as follows:

RASHI: "It is the finger of the Lord"— This plague is not done by sorcery, but it comes from God.

CASSUTO: They admitted that there was here a greater power than theirs, and that Moshe and Aaron were not acting on their own, as they [the sorcerers] acted on their own power.... But their recogni-tion was only a partial recognition. They did not say "the finger of God (ה')", but "the finger of the Lord (אלהים)." They did not yet recognize the Divine Providence of God (ה'—the God of Israel), but just acknowledged the existence of a Divine power. And they also did not say "the hand of the Lord," but just "the finger of the Lord," meaning that they did not admit to the full force of the Divine power.

רַבִּי עֲקִיבָא אוֹמֵר: מִנַּיִן שֶׁכָּל־מַכָּה וּמַכָּה, שֶׁהֵבִיא הַקָּדוֹשׁ בָּרוּךְ הוּא עַל הַמִּצְרִים בְּמִצְרַיִם, הָיְתָה שֶׁל חָמֵשׁ מַכּוֹת? שֶׁנֶּאֱמַר: יְשַׁלַּח־בָּם חֲרוֹן אַפּוֹ, עֶבְרָה וָזַעַם וְצָרָה. מִשְׁלַחַת מַלְאֲכֵי רָעִים. חֲרוֹן אַפּוֹ אַחַת. עֶבְרָה שְׁתַּיִם. וָזַעַם שָׁלֹשׁ. וְצָרָה אַרְבַּע. מִשְׁלַחַת מַלְאֲכֵי רָעִים חָמֵשׁ: אֱמוֹר מֵעַתָּה, בְּמִצְרַיִם לָקוּ חֲמִשִּׁים מַכּוֹת, וְעַל הַיָּם לָקוּ חֲמִשִּׁים וּמָאתַיִם מַכּוֹת:

RASHBAM: It is a natural plague, and not performed by these men—for if it was done by sorcery, we could also have done it.

Questions

1) Explain how we can understand the reaction of the sorcerers to the plague of lice according to these three commentators.

2) How does Cassuto explain the use of the two names of God in this section?

3) How does Cassuto's commentary support *Abarbanel*'s explanation of Rabbi Yehuda's division of the plagues above?

4) What part of Casssuto's explanation serves as a basis for the *drashot* of Rabbi Yossi, Rabbi Eliezer and Rabbi Akiva?

Suggested Answers

1) According to *Rashi* and Cassuto, the sorcerers' reaction represents a recognition of God. According to *Rashbam*, it is merely a recognition that the plagues are beyond human control and are a phenomena of nature.

2) The use of the name "אלהים" by the sorcerers in their reaction to the plague of lice, as opposed to the name "ה'," which is used prevalently in the entire section, indicates that they recognized the existence of a God, but not specifically the God of *Bnai Yisrael*.

Rabbi Akiva said: *How do we know that each individual plague which the Holy One Blessed be He brought upon the Egyptians in Egypt consisted of five plagues? For it says (Tehillim 78:49): "He sent upon them his fierce anger: wrath, fury, trouble, and a team of hostile angels." Fierce anger is one, wrath is two, fury is three, trouble is four and a team of hostile angels is five. From here we can conclude that in Egypt they were struck by 50 plagues, and at the sea they were struck by 250 plagues.*

3) *Abarbanel* suggested that the first three plagues were brought to arouse in Pharaoh and the Egyptians a recognition of God's existence. The statement of the sorcerers after the third plague (the last plague of the first group) indicates that this goal was realized. The sorcerers are no longer a part of the story after this point as they recognize that the plagues are the result of a Divine power that goes beyond the scope of their capability.

4) Cassuto points out two differences in language between the statement of the sorcerers after the plague of lice and the statement at the sea: "And Israel saw the great hand which God laid upon the Egyptians...." One difference, that of the names of God, is addressed in answer three. The second difference is that the sorcerers refer to the **"finger of the Lord"** while the verse at the sea refers to the **"hand of God."**

According to Cassuto, this indicates that the sorcerers did not recognize the full force of God's power since the show of force at the sea was greater than it was in Egypt. This comparison is the basis for the explanations of Rabbi Yossi, Rabbi Eliezer, and Rabbi Akiva in the Haggadah—that the show of force at the sea was five times greater than the show of force in Egypt (the ratio of one finger to an entire hand).

כַּמָּה מַעֲלוֹת טוֹבוֹת לַמָּקוֹם עָלֵינוּ:

אִלּוּ הוֹצִיאָנוּ מִמִּצְרַיִם, וְלֹא עָשָׂה בָהֶם שְׁפָטִים, **דַּיֵּנוּ:**

אִלּוּ עָשָׂה בָהֶם שְׁפָטִים, וְלֹא עָשָׂה בֵאלֹהֵיהֶם, **דַּיֵּנוּ:**

אִלּוּ עָשָׂה בֵאלֹהֵיהֶם, וְלֹא הָרַג אֶת־בְּכוֹרֵיהֶם, **דַּיֵּנוּ:**

אִלּוּ הָרַג אֶת־בְּכוֹרֵיהֶם, וְלֹא נָתַן לָנוּ אֶת־מָמוֹנָם, **דַּיֵּנוּ:**

אִלּוּ נָתַן לָנוּ אֶת־מָמוֹנָם, וְלֹא קָרַע לָנוּ אֶת־הַיָּם, **דַּיֵּנוּ:**

אִלּוּ קָרַע לָנוּ אֶת־הַיָּם, וְלֹא הֶעֱבִירָנוּ בְתוֹכוֹ בֶּחָרָבָה, **דַּיֵּנוּ:**

אִלּוּ הֶעֱבִירָנוּ בְתוֹכוֹ בֶּחָרָבָה, וְלֹא שִׁקַּע צָרֵינוּ בְּתוֹכוֹ, **דַּיֵּנוּ:**

אִלּוּ שִׁקַּע צָרֵינוּ בְּתוֹכוֹ,

וְלֹא סִפֵּק צָרְכֵּנוּ בַּמִּדְבָּר אַרְבָּעִים שָׁנָה, **דַּיֵּנוּ:**

אִלּוּ סִפֵּק צָרְכֵּנוּ בַּמִּדְבָּר אַרְבָּעִים שָׁנָה,

וְלֹא הֶאֱכִילָנוּ אֶת־הַמָּן, **דַּיֵּנוּ:**

אִלּוּ הֶאֱכִילָנוּ אֶת־הַמָּן, וְלֹא נָתַן לָנוּ אֶת־הַשַּׁבָּת, **דַּיֵּנוּ:**

אִלּוּ נָתַן לָנוּ אֶת־הַשַּׁבָּת, וְלֹא קֵרְבָנוּ לִפְנֵי הַר סִינַי, **דַּיֵּנוּ:**

אִלּוּ קֵרְבָנוּ לִפְנֵי הַר סִינַי, וְלֹא נָתַן לָנוּ אֶת־הַתּוֹרָה, **דַּיֵּנוּ:**

אִלּוּ נָתַן לָנוּ אֶת־הַתּוֹרָה, וְלֹא הִכְנִיסָנוּ לְאֶרֶץ יִשְׂרָאֵל, **דַּיֵּנוּ:**

אִלּוּ הִכְנִיסָנוּ לְאֶרֶץ יִשְׂרָאֵל,

וְלֹא בָנָה לָנוּ אֶת־בֵּית הַבְּחִירָה, **דַּיֵּנוּ:**

So many levels of favors has God bestowed upon us:

Had He brought us out from Egypt, and not executed judgment
against the Egyptians,   ***it would have been enough for us!***

Had He executed judgments against them,
and not against their gods,   ***it would have been enough for us!***

Had He executed judgment against their gods,
and not smitten their firstborn,   ***it would have been enough for us!***

Had He slain their firstborn,
and had not given us their wealth,   ***it would have been enough for us!***

Had He given us their wealth,
and not split the sea for us,   ***it would have been enough for us!***

Had He split the sea for us,
and not led us through it on dry land,   ***it would have been enough for us!***

Had He led us through on dry land,
and not drowned our tormenters in it,   ***it would have been enough for us!***

Had He drowned our tormenters in it, and not provided for our
needs in the desert for forty years,   ***it would have been enough for us!***

Had He provided for our needs in the desert for forty years,
and not fed us the manna,   ***it would have been enough for us!***

Had He fed us the manna,
and not given us the Shabbat,   ***it would have been enough for us!***

Had He given us the Shabbat, and not brought us
before Mount Sinai,   ***it would have been enough for us!***

Had He brought us before Mount Sinai,
and not given us the Torah,   ***it would have been enough for us!***

Had He given us the Torah, and not brought us
into the Land of Israel,   ***it would have been enough for us!***

Had He brought us into the Land of Israel,
and not built the Holy Temple,   ***it would have been enough for us!***

עַל אַחַת כַּמָּה וְכַמָּה טוֹבָה כְפוּלָה וּמְכֻפֶּלֶת לַמָּקוֹם עָלֵינוּ:
שֶׁהוֹצִיאָנוּ מִמִּצְרַיִם, וְעָשָׂה בָהֶם שְׁפָטִים, וְעָשָׂה בֵאלֹהֵיהֶם,
וְהָרַג אֶת־בְּכוֹרֵיהֶם, וְנָתַן לָנוּ אֶת־מָמוֹנָם, וְקָרַע לָנוּ אֶת־
הַיָּם, וְהֶעֱבִירָנוּ בְתוֹכוֹ בֶּחָרָבָה, וְשִׁקַּע צָרֵינוּ בְּתוֹכוֹ, וְסִפֵּק
צָרְכֵּנוּ בַּמִּדְבָּר אַרְבָּעִים שָׁנָה, וְהֶאֱכִילָנוּ אֶת־הַמָּן, וְנָתַן לָנוּ
אֶת־הַשַּׁבָּת, וְקֵרְבָנוּ לִפְנֵי הַר סִינַי, וְנָתַן לָנוּ אֶת־הַתּוֹרָה,
וְהִכְנִיסָנוּ לְאֶרֶץ יִשְׂרָאֵל, וּבָנָה לָנוּ אֶת־בֵּית הַבְּחִירָה, לְכַפֵּר
עַל־כָּל־עֲוֹנוֹתֵינוּ.

"IF HE WOULD HAVE BROUGHT US BEFORE MOUNT SINAI, BUT NOT GIVEN US THE TORAH, IT WOULD HAVE SUFFICED FOR US."

MIDRASH RABBAH (*Kohelet* 3:15): What is it like?—It is like a king whose son recovered from an illness. They said to him: "Let your son go to his school." He replied: "My son has not yet regained his splendor, and you suggest that he go to his school? Let him relax for two or three months to eat and drink and convalesce, and afterward he will go to school." Thus said God: "My children have not yet recovered their splendor from the mud and bricks that they left, and I should give them the Torah? Let them relax for two or three months with the *manna* [see *Shemot* 16:4–6], the well and the quail,

and afterward I will give them the Torah." When? In the third month.

MIDRASH TANCHUMA (*Yitro* 10): Rav Yehudah the son of Shalom said: It is like the son of a king who recovered from an illness. His father said: "We will wait three months until his spirit returns to him and then I will take him to the Rav to learn Torah." So too, when Israel left Egypt, there were those among them who were blemished by the bondage. God said: "I will wait until they heal and after that I will give them the Torah."

Thus how much more so should we be grateful to God for the manifold goodness that He has showered upon us; for He brought us out of Egypt; and executed judgments against them and against their gods, and slew their firstborn; and gave us their wealth; and split the sea for us; and led us through it on dry land; and drowned our tormenters in it, and provided for our needs in the desert for forty years, and fed us the manna, and gave us the Shabbat; and brought us before Mount Sinai; and gave us the Torah; and brought us into the land of Israel; and built for us the Holy Temple to atone for all our sins.

Questions

1) **What is the question that lies behind these two midrashim?**

2) **What is the idea that is communicated by the midrashim? Is there a difference between them?**

Suggested Answers

1) Why was the Torah not given to them immediately upon their departure from Egypt, particularly when Moshe had been told: "When you take them out of Egypt, you will worship God on this mountain"? (*Shemot* 3:12)

2) Both midrashim indicate that *Bnai Yisrael* needed time to recover from the effects of the Egyptian bondage before they would be able to receive the Torah. According to *Midrash Tanchuma*, it was a physical recovery. According to *Midrash Rabbah*, it included also a spiritual recovery, as indicated by the mention of the *manna* which included prohibitions and was designated as a test of the faith of *Bnai Yisrael* (see *Shemot* 16:4–6). Thus, there was a value in the three months break prior to *Bnai Yisrael* receiving the Torah. In this sense, if we had been brought to Mount Sinai and not received the Torah, it would have been sufficient.

רַבָּן גַּמְלִיאֵל הָיָה אוֹמֵר: כָּל שֶׁלֹּא אָמַר שְׁלֹשָׁה דְבָרִים אֵלּוּ
בַּפֶּסַח, לֹא יָצָא יְדֵי חוֹבָתוֹ, וְאֵלּוּ הֵן:

פֶּסַח. מַצָּה. וּמָרוֹר:

פֶּסַח שֶׁהָיוּ אֲבוֹתֵינוּ אוֹכְלִים, בִּזְמַן שֶׁבֵּית הַמִּקְדָשׁ הָיָה
קַיָּם, עַל שׁוּם מָה? עַל שׁוּם שֶׁפָּסַח הַקָּדוֹשׁ בָּרוּךְ
הוּא, עַל בָּתֵּי אֲבוֹתֵינוּ בְּמִצְרַיִם, שֶׁנֶּאֱמַר: וַאֲמַרְתֶּם זֶבַח פֶּסַח
הוּא לַיְיָ, אֲשֶׁר פָּסַח עַל בָּתֵּי בְנֵי יִשְׂרָאֵל בְּמִצְרַיִם, בְּנָגְפּוֹ
אֶת־מִצְרַיִם וְאֶת־בָּתֵּינוּ הִצִּיל, וַיִּקֹּד הָעָם וַיִּשְׁתַּחֲווּ:

BECAUSE GOD PASSED OVER

RABBAN GAMLIEL suggests that the Pesach sacrifice observed by *Bnai Yisrael* throughout the generations was reminiscent of the role that the sacrifice played in God passing over the houses of *Bnai Yisrael* in Egypt during the plague of the killing of the firstborn. A number of commentators have discussed this relationship:

RAMBAM: The Egyptians were accustomed to worshiping the zodiacal sign of the lamb. That was why they forbade the slaughter of cattle and despised shepherds.... For this reason, we were commanded to slaughter a lamb on Pesach and sprinkle its blood in Egypt on the doors outside—to cleanse ourselves of these ideas and demonstrate publicly our

Rabban Gamliel used to say: Whoever does not discuss the following three things on Pesach has not fulfilled his obligation, and these are:

Pesach, Matzah and Maror

The Pesach sacrifice *that our fathers ate during the period of the Holy Temple—what is its meaning? Because the Holy One blessed be He passed over our fathers' houses in Egypt, as it says: "You shall say, 'It is a Pesach sacrifice to the Lord who passed over the houses of the Children of Israel in Egypt when He smote the Egyptians and saved our houses.' And the people bowed down and prostrated themselves." (Shemot 12:27)*

rejection of them.... The Lord passed over the doorways and did not allow the destroyer to enter your houses and to do you harm—in reward for your performance of rites repugnant to the worshipers of idols.

HAKETAV VEHAKABBALAH: If they [*Bnai Yisrael*] were willing to place their lives in danger in order to carry out the wishes of the Almighty, that would be a true token of their love of God. Conse-

quently, God commanded them to slay the Egyptian god in full view of all. First they had to procure the lamb and lead it through the streets without fear of Egyptian reaction. Second they had to slaughter it family by family, in groups. And finally they had to sprinkle its blood on the doorposts for every Egyptian passerby to see, braving the vengeance of their former persecutors. Their fulfillment of every detail of this ritual would be proof of their complete faith in God.

AKEIDAT YITZCHAK: Laying one's hands on a sheep or a goat was sacrilege in the eyes of the Egyptians. The Egyptians would suddenly be confronted by the spectacle of their downtrodden slaves having the audacity to take hold of the gods that they worshiped, the lamb.... Then with the Egyptians powerlessly looking on, the blood of the slaughtered animals would be publicly displayed on the doorposts.... The lamb was considered by the Egyptian astrologers to be one of the most favorable signs of the zodiac, under which the Egyptian people lived. On the tenth of the month, that is at the beginning of its reign, they would witness its downfall before it had run more than a third of its course. And on the fourteenth day, when it was at the height of its strength, it would be slaughtered and eaten.

Questions

1) What misunderstanding regarding the placing of the blood on the doorpost do these commentaries want to prevent?

2) What is the difference between their explanations of the reason for the Pesach offering in Egypt?

3) What other details of the Pesach offering in Egypt (other than the placing of the blood on the doorpost) are explained by these commentaries?*

4) The following is an excerpt from the explanation of Rabbi Shimshon Raphael Hirsch:

> The blood of the sacrifice was to be placed on the lintel and the doorposts symbolizing the home within which the sacrifice would be eaten. The concept of the home comprises two elements, social protection from society and physical protection from the forces of nature.... The slave liberated from the Egyptian bondage... was rewarded with doorposts and a lintel, Divine protection against human and natural forces.

How does Hirsch's explanation differ from the three explanations quoted above?

---

* You might find the following verses helpful in answering this question:
"Speak to all of the congregation of Israel saying: 'On the tenth day of this month every man shall take a lamb, according to the house of their fathers, a lamb for a house. And if the household be too small for a lamb, let him and his nearby neighbor take it according to the number of souls.... And you shall keep it until the fourteenth day of the same month, and the whole assembly of the congregation of Israel shall kill it toward evening. And they shall take the blood and put it on the two doorposts and on the lintel of the houses in which they will eat it.'" (*Shemot* 12:3–7)

Suggested Answers

1) All three commentators are trying to dispel the possible misunderstanding that God needed to see the blood on the doorposts in order to know which homes to pass over. Certainly, God would know which homes to pass over without any need of a sign.

2) *Rambam* contends that *Bnai Yisrael* had to free themselves from idolatrous practices and ideas before they would be worthy of being redeemed. *Haketav Vehakabbalah* claims that they had to free themselves of their fear of the Egyptians in order to be worthy of redemption. Thus, according to both of these commentators, the Pesach offering and the placement of the blood on the doorpost were acts that they did for their own growth. The blood demonstrated their worthiness to be redeemed.

Akeidat Yitzchak's focus is more on the impact of these acts on the Egyptians. The offering and the placing of the blood were defiant acts that demonstrated to the Egyptians the illegitimacy of their beliefs. This expresses the idea that we have seen previously (pages 67–68) regarding the importance of destroying their ideology as a means toward weakening them physically.

3) The following are explanations of some of the mitzvot related to the Pesach offering in Egypt:

The lamb had to be taken four days before it was to be slaughtered, led through the streets and kept in the house to make the act more of a public demonstration.

The two dates, the tenth (the day of the taking) and the fourteenth (the day of the slaughtering) are related to the cycle of the zodiac. In conjunction with the cycle of the moon, the lamb is increasing in power at the tenth and reaches its peak on the fourteenth. This increased the adverse impact of the slaughtering in the eyes of the Egyptians.

Eating the Pesach offering in groups increased the public nature of the event.

4) According to Hirsch, the placing of the blood did not relate to the status of *Bnai Yisrael* **before** the redemption, but rather to their status **after** the redemption—to the Divine protection that they were destined to receive.

Lift up the matzah and recite the following:

מַ**צָּ**ה זוֹ שֶׁאָנוּ אוֹכְלִים, עַל שׁוּם מָה? עַל שׁוּם שֶׁלֹּא
הִסְפִּיק בְּצֵקָם שֶׁל אֲבוֹתֵינוּ לְהַחֲמִיץ, עַד שֶׁנִּגְלָה
עֲלֵיהֶם מֶלֶךְ מַלְכֵי הַמְּלָכִים, הַקָּדוֹשׁ בָּרוּךְ הוּא, וּגְאָלָם,
שֶׁנֶּאֱמַר: וַיֹּאפוּ אֶת־הַבָּצֵק, אֲשֶׁר הוֹצִיאוּ מִמִּצְרַיִם, עֻגֹת
מַצּוֹת, כִּי לֹא חָמֵץ: כִּי גֹרְשׁוּ מִמִּצְרַיִם, וְלֹא יָכְלוּ לְהִתְמַהְמֵהַּ,
וְגַם צֵדָה לֹא עָשׂוּ לָהֶם.

"BECAUSE THEY WERE DRIVEN OUT OF EGYPT"

RAMBAN (Shemot 12:39): And they baked the dough: They baked it into matzah because of the mitzvah that they were commanded: "No leaven shall be found in your house" (Shemot 12:19). And it states "because they were driven out of Egypt" to say that they baked it on the way because they were forced out of Egypt and could not wait to bake it in the city and to carry it as matzot...and they hurried and baked it before it became leavened on the way....

BA'AL HATURIM (Shemot 12:39): And they baked the dough: As its simple meaning: "Because they were driven from Egypt" is the reason that they baked matzah. If they had remained, they would have let it rise because for the Pesach in Egypt they were only commanded to eat matzah on the first night.

SHADAL (Shemot 12:21): Behold in this

section (verses 21–28), Moshe did not mention to Israel at all the issue of eating matzah and the prohibition of chametz even though it was mentioned in the section above (verse 12:19), because he knew that they would be driven out and their dough would not have time to rise. And Moshe did not say anything about this because they would not have been able to understand why they were eating matzah. Only after they went out did he specify the prohibition of chametz and the mitzvah of matzah, because then they could understand that it is as a remembrance of the miracle that they were driven out of Egypt and could not wait.... Nevertheless, it appears that he did tell them to eat the Pesach offering with matzah and bitter herbs. And the eating of the Pesach sacrifice with matzah is apparently also related to hurrying, that they had to eat it in a hurry.

Lift up the matzah and recite the following:

This matzah that we eat—*what is its meaning? It is because our fathers' dough did not have time to rise before the King of kings: the Holy One Blessed be He revealed Himself to them and redeemed them. As it says: "They baked the dough which they had brought out of Egypt into cakes of matzah, for it had not leavened; because they were driven out of Egypt and could not delay, nor had they prepared provisions for themselves." (Shemot 12:39)*

Questions

℟1) **What is the question that the commentators are trying to resolve?**

℟℟2) **How many responses are given by the three commentators above, and what are the differences between them?**

3) **Which explanation is reflected in the Haggadah?**

4) **What is the difference between *Ramban* and *Shadal* in their interpretation of the phrase "because they were driven out of Egypt"?**

Suggested Answers

1) There seems to be an inconsistency in the text regarding the eating of matzah. In verse 12:29, the Torah records the mitzvah of eating matzah for seven days. Yet, twenty verses later it states that *Bnai Yisrael* baked matzah "because they were driven from Egypt" and did not have time to allow the dough to rise. Were they com-

manded to eat matzah, or was it determined by circumstances?

2) There are essentially two opinions expressed by the three commentators:

ACCORDING TO RAMBAN: they ate the matzah because they were commanded to. Verse 39 merely tells us that they baked the matzot on the way rather than in Egypt because they were driven out.

BA'AL HATURIM AND SHADAL both say that they were not commanded to eat matzah in Egypt for seven days. According to *Ba'al Haturim*, they were commanded to do so only on the first night, while according to *Shadal*, they were commanded to eat the Pesach sacrifice with matzah. Nevertheless, the matzah that was baked on the way was a matter of circumstance. The prohibition of eating chametz for seven days was instituted for the generations after the Exodus as a remembrance of this event. Shadal supports his

The *maror* is held up and the following passage is recited:

מָרוֹר זֶה שֶׁאָנוּ אוֹכְלִים, עַל שׁוּם מָה? עַל שׁוּם שֶׁמֵּרְרוּ הַמִּצְרִים אֶת־חַיֵּי אֲבוֹתֵינוּ בְּמִצְרָיִם, שֶׁנֶּאֱמַר: וַיְמָרֲרוּ אֶת־חַיֵּיהֶם בַּעֲבֹדָה קָשָׁה, בְּחֹמֶר וּבִלְבֵנִים, וּבְכָל־עֲבֹדָה בַּשָּׂדֶה: אֵת כָּל־עֲבֹדָתָם, אֲשֶׁר עָבְדוּ בָהֶם בְּפָרֶךְ.

position by pointing out that Moshe did not mention the prohibition of chametz to the people.

3) The position of *Ba'al Haturim* and *Shadal* is reflected in the Haggadah, which describes the matzah as a remembrance of the fact that they were driven from Egypt and did not have time for the dough to rise.

4) The difference between Ramban and *Shadal* in their interpretation of the phrase "because they were driven out of Egypt" relates to the part of the verse it modifies. According to Ramban, it refers to the phrase "and they baked the dough that they brought out of Egypt." That is to say that they would have baked the matzah in Egypt had they not been driven out. According to Shadal, it modifies the phrase "for it had not leavened." In other words, they would have allowed the dough to rise and become bread had they not been driven out and forced to bake it in a hurry. Thus, the verse would read as follows according to each commentator:

RAMBAN: And they baked the dough that they had brought out of Egypt because they were driven out and could not delay, unleavened bread that did not rise....

SHADAL: And they baked the dough that they had brought out of Egypt, unleavened bread that did not rise because they were driven out and could not delay.

CHAG HAPESACH

Passover is referred to in the Torah as "the holiday of Pesach" (חג הפסח) and as "the holiday of unleavened bread" (חג המצות):

On the fourteenth day of the month at dusk, is God's Passover. (*Vayikra* 23:5)

And on the fifteenth day of the same month is the feast of unleavened bread to the Lord; seven days you shall eat unleavened bread.

(*Vayikra* 23:6)

The *maror* is held up and the following passage is recited:

This bitter herb that we eat—*what is its meaning? Because the Egyptians embittered our fathers' lives in Egypt, as it says: "They made their lives bitter with hard labor, with mortar and with bricks, and with all manner of labor in the field; whatever they made them do was with rigor." (Shemot 1:14)*

Question
What is the reason for the change in the name of the holiday?

Suggested Answer
The first verse refers to the first night of the holiday on which the Pesach sacrifice was brought. The remaining days of the holiday have no relationship to the Pesach sacrifice. The matzah, however, relates to all seven days of the holiday, since they were hurrying to evade the Egyptians during that entire period. Therefore, the second verse, which refers to all seven days, utilizes the expression "holiday of unleavened bread."

THIS BITTER HERB THAT WE EAT

As indicated previously, *Ibn Ezra* interpreted the word "with rigor" (בפרך) to refer to work that was enforced by the Egyptians on *Bnai Yisrael* beyond the normal standards of servitude. According to Nechama, this idea is further developed in this verse. The closing phrase "all of their work that they made them do was with rigor" seems superfluous since the verse already mentioned the hard work that they were forced to do in building and in the field. This indicates that not only were *Bnai Yisrael* slaves to Pharaoh, but they were forced to do the work of the common Egyptians ("their work"–עבודתם). This is reflected in the fact that the tenth plague effected even the firstborn of the Egyptian maidservants ("from the firstborn of Pharaoh who sits on his throne to the firstborn of the maidservants"—"מבכור פרעה הישב על כסאו עד בכור השפחה"—*Shemot* 11:5). *Rashi* explains that the firstborn children of the maidservants were struck down because they forced *Bnai Yisrael* to work and were happy with their affliction. The bitterness of the bondage in Egypt was heightened by the fact that they were not only oppressed by the government, but by all strands of the Egyptian society.

בְּכָל־דּוֹר וָדוֹר חַיָּב אָדָם לִרְאוֹת אֶת־עַצְמוֹ, כְּאִלּוּ הוּא יָצָא מִמִּצְרַיִם, שֶׁנֶּאֱמַר: וְהִגַּדְתָּ לְבִנְךָ בַּיּוֹם הַהוּא לֵאמֹר: בַּעֲבוּר זֶה עָשָׂה יְיָ לִי, בְּצֵאתִי מִמִּצְרָיִם. לֹא אֶת־אֲבוֹתֵינוּ בִּלְבַד, גָּאַל הַקָּדוֹשׁ בָּרוּךְ הוּא, אֶלָּא אַף אוֹתָנוּ גָּאַל עִמָּהֶם, שֶׁנֶּאֱמַר: וְאוֹתָנוּ הוֹצִיא מִשָּׁם, לְמַעַן הָבִיא אֹתָנוּ, לָתֶת לָנוּ אֶת־הָאָרֶץ אֲשֶׁר נִשְׁבַּע לַאֲבֹתֵינוּ.

IN EVERY GENERATION

Questions

1) Where in the verse (from *Shemot*) that is cited do we find a hint that in every generation one must see himself as if he went out of Egypt?

2) Where else do we find this idea in the Torah?

Suggested Answers

1) The verse referring to the obligation to transmit the story of the Exodus to one's children throughout the generations surprisingly refers to the events in the first person singular ("what God did for **me** when He took **me** out of Egypt"). It would have been grammatically more appropriate for the verse to have used the third person plural ("what God did for them") or the first person plural ("what God did for us"). The use of the first person singular personalizes the events, indicating the obligation to relive them in every generation.

2) In addressing *Bnai Yisrael* prior to his death, Moshe uses the following terminology: "The Lord our God made a covenant with us at Horev. The Lord did not make this covenant with our fathers, but with us who are alive here today." A few verses later, Moshe repeats the Ten Commandments, which are interestingly also written in the first person singular: "I am the Lord your (sing.) God who brought you (sing.) out of the land of Egypt."

In every generation, *it is one's duty to see himself as though he had personally come out from Egypt, as it says: "You shall tell your son on that day: 'It was because of this that the Lord did [all these miracles] for me when I went out of Egypt' (Shemot 13:8)." Not only our fathers did the Holy One Blessed be He redeem from Egypt, but He redeemed us with them as well, as it says: "It was us that He brought out from there, so that He might bring us to give us the land that He promised to our fathers." (Devarim 6:23)*

In her *Gilayon* for *Bo* 5716, Nechama quoted the unique position of Harav Avraham Yitzchak Hacohen Kook regarding the ongoing nature of the Exodus from Egypt. According to Harav Kook, the Exodus from Egypt was fundamentally the struggle of the Jew to overcome his secular nature and to achieve sanctity. He explained the mitzvah of wearing tefillin on the arm as follows: just as God needed a strong hand to extricate *Bnai Yisrael* from Egypt, so too in every generation the individual Jew needs a strong hand in order to extricate himself from his "personal Egypt."

Raise the cup of wine.

לְפִיכָךְ אֲנַחְנוּ חַיָּבִים לְהוֹדוֹת, לְהַלֵּל, לְשַׁבֵּחַ, לְפָאֵר, לְרוֹמֵם, לְהַדֵּר, לְבָרֵךְ, לְעַלֵּה וּלְקַלֵּס, לְמִי שֶׁעָשָׂה לַאֲבוֹתֵינוּ וְלָנוּ אֶת־כָּל־הַנִּסִּים הָאֵלּוּ. הוֹצִיאָנוּ מֵעַבְדוּת לְחֵרוּת, מִיָּגוֹן לְשִׂמְחָה, וּמֵאֵבֶל לְיוֹם טוֹב, וּמֵאֲפֵלָה לְאוֹר גָּדוֹל, וּמִשִּׁעְבּוּד לִגְאֻלָּה. וְנֹאמַר לְפָנָיו שִׁירָה חֲדָשָׁה. הַלְלוּיָהּ:

הַלְלוּיָהּ. הַלְלוּ עַבְדֵי יְיָ. הַלְלוּ אֶת־שֵׁם יְיָ. יְהִי שֵׁם יְיָ מְבֹרָךְ מֵעַתָּה וְעַד עוֹלָם: מִמִּזְרַח שֶׁמֶשׁ עַד מְבוֹאוֹ. מְהֻלָּל שֵׁם יְיָ. רָם עַל־כָּל־גּוֹיִם יְיָ. עַל הַשָּׁמַיִם כְּבוֹדוֹ: מִי כַּיְיָ אֱלֹהֵינוּ. הַמַּגְבִּיהִי לָשָׁבֶת: הַמַּשְׁפִּילִי לִרְאוֹת בַּשָּׁמַיִם וּבָאָרֶץ: מְקִימִי מֵעָפָר דָּל. מֵאַשְׁפֹּת יָרִים אֶבְיוֹן: לְהוֹשִׁיבִי עִם־נְדִיבִים. עִם נְדִיבֵי עַמּוֹ: מוֹשִׁיבִי עֲקֶרֶת הַבַּיִת אֵם הַבָּנִים שְׂמֵחָה. הַלְלוּיָהּ:

AN ETHICAL AND THEOLOGICAL IMPERATIVE

The above paragraph, which concludes the Maggid section of the Haggadah, brings together, as well, several of the strands that we have seen in Nechama's teachings. The performance of the Seder, including the engaging discussion and analysis of the Exodus (סיפור ביציאת מצרים), is designed to have us relive the liberation from Egypt annually. This experience engenders both an ethical imperative and a theological imperative. Nechama related to both in her *Studies in Shemot*:

1) **The Ethical Imperative**—Nechama pointed out that the Torah cautions us regarding our behavior toward the stranger no less than 36 times, the most repeated injunction in the Torah. According to *Rashi* (*Shemot* 23:9), this imperative flows from our experience in Egypt: "You know the feelings of the stranger—how painful it is for him when you oppress him." Empathy is an outgrowth of experience. Nechama summarized as follows: "We are bidden to put ourselves in the

Raise the cup of wine.

Therefore *it is our duty to thank, praise, hail, glorify, exalt, honor, bless, extol and celebrate Him Who did all these miracles for our fathers and us. He brought us forth from slavery to freedom, from sorrow to joy, and from mourning to festivity, and from darkness to great light, and from servitude to redemption. Let us therefore recite before Him a new song: Halleluyah!*

Halleluyah! *Praise His mighty deeds, you servants of the Lord, praise the Name of God. Blessed be the Name of the Lord from now and forever. From the rising of the sun to its setting, praised be the Name of the Lord. Supreme above all nations is the Lord, above the heavens is His glory. Who is like the Lord, our God, Who is enthroned on high, yet looks down upon the heaven and the earth? He raises the poor from the dust, from the trash heaps He lifts the pauper—to seat them with nobles, with the nobles of His people. He transforms a childless woman into a joyful mother of children. Halleluyah.*

position of the stranger by remembering how it felt when we were strangers in another land."*

2) The Theological Imperative—The first of the Ten Commandments reads: "I am the Lord your God who took you out of the land of Egypt…." (*Shemot* 20:2) Nechama cited the question of Yehuda Halevi as to why the verse identifies God through reference to the Exodus from Egypt rather than by reference to the creation of the world? She paraphrased his response as follows: "Fundamental for Halevi is the distinction between Aristotle's God to whom speculation alone

conduces, and the God of Avraham for whom the soul yearns…. For Halevi, faith in the Creator of philosophical theology is inferior to the religious experience of God's miracles."** The experience of the Seder is, thus, also designed to lead us to the recognition of God inherent in the ten plagues, the splitting of the sea, and the four expressions of redemption:

וידעתם כי אני ה' אלהיכם המוציא אתכם
מתחת סבלות מצרים

And you shall know that I am the Lord your God who takes you out from under the burdens of Egypt.

(*Shemot* 6:7)

---

* Leibowitz, Nechama, *Studies in Shemot* (Jerusalem: WZO, 1976) pp. 380–83.
**Ibid., pp. 308–10.

בְּצֵאת יִשְׂרָאֵל מִמִּצְרָיִם, בֵּית יַעֲקֹב מֵעַם לֹעֵז: הָיְתָה יְהוּדָה לְקָדְשׁוֹ. יִשְׂרָאֵל מַמְשְׁלוֹתָיו: הַיָּם רָאָה וַיָּנֹס, הַיַּרְדֵּן יִסֹּב לְאָחוֹר: הֶהָרִים רָקְדוּ כְאֵילִים. גְּבָעוֹת כִּבְנֵי־צֹאן: מַה־לְּךָ הַיָּם כִּי תָנוּס. הַיַּרְדֵּן תִּסֹּב לְאָחוֹר: הֶהָרִים תִּרְקְדוּ כְאֵילִים. גְּבָעוֹת כִּבְנֵי־צֹאן: מִלִּפְנֵי אָדוֹן חוּלִי אָרֶץ. מִלִּפְנֵי אֱלוֹהַ יַעֲקֹב: הַהֹפְכִי הַצּוּר אֲגַם־מָיִם. חַלָּמִישׁ לְמַעְיְנוֹ־מָיִם.

The matzot are covered and the cup is lifted.

בָּרוּךְ אַתָּה יְיָ, אֱלֹהֵינוּ מֶלֶךְ הָעוֹלָם, אֲשֶׁר גְּאָלָנוּ וְגָאַל אֶת־אֲבוֹתֵינוּ מִמִּצְרַיִם, וְהִגִּיעָנוּ לַלַּיְלָה הַזֶּה, לֶאֱכָל־בּוֹ מַצָּה וּמָרוֹר. כֵּן, יְיָ אֱלֹהֵינוּ וֵאלֹהֵי אֲבוֹתֵינוּ, יַגִּיעֵנוּ לְמוֹעֲדִים וְלִרְגָלִים אֲחֵרִים, הַבָּאִים לִקְרָאתֵנוּ לְשָׁלוֹם. שְׂמֵחִים בְּבִנְיַן עִירֶךָ, וְשָׂשִׂים בַּעֲבוֹדָתֶךָ, וְנֹאכַל שָׁם מִן הַזְּבָחִים וּמִן הַפְּסָחִים (במוצאי שבת אומרים מִן הַפְּסָחִים וּמִן הַזְּבָחִים), אֲשֶׁר יַגִּיעַ דָּמָם, עַל קִיר מִזְבַּחֲךָ לְרָצוֹן, וְנוֹדֶה לְךָ שִׁיר חָדָשׁ עַל גְּאֻלָּתֵנוּ, וְעַל פְּדוּת נַפְשֵׁנוּ: בָּרוּךְ אַתָּה יְיָ, גָּאַל יִשְׂרָאֵל:

בָּרוּךְ אַתָּה יְיָ, אֱלֹהֵינוּ מֶלֶךְ הָעוֹלָם, בּוֹרֵא פְּרִי הַגָּפֶן:

The second cup is drunk while leaning on the left side.

When Israel went out from Egypt, *the House of Yaakov from a people of a foreign language, Judah became His holy one, Israel His dominion. The sea saw and fled; the Jordan turned backward. The mountains skipped like rams, the hills like young sheep. What ails you, sea, that you flee, Jordan, that you turn backward? Mountains, why do you skip like rams, hills, like young sheep? Tremble O earth before the God of Yaakov, who turns the rock into a pool of water, the flint into a flowing fountain.*

The matzot are covered and the cup is lifted.

Blessed are You, Lord our God, King of the universe, *who has redeemed us and redeemed our fathers from Egypt, and enabled us to reach this night that we may eat matzah and maror on it. So too, Lord our God and God of our fathers, enable us to reach future holidays and festivals in peace, rejoicing in the rebuilding of Your city and ecstatic in Your service. And there we will partake of the sacrifices and Pesach offerings [on Saturday night say: of the Pesach offerings and of the sacrifices] whose blood shall be sprinkled on the wall of Your altar for gracious acceptance. We will then thank You with a new song for our redemption and for the deliverance of our souls. Blessed are You, God, who has redeemed Israel.*

Blessed are You, Lord our God, King of the universe, who creates the fruit of the vine.

The second cup is drunk while leaning on the left side.

℠ רָחְצָה ℞

The participants wash their hands and then recite the following blessing:

בָּרוּךְ אַתָּה יְיָ אֱלֹהֵינוּ מֶלֶךְ הָעוֹלָם, אֲשֶׁר קִדְּשָׁנוּ בְּמִצְוֹתָיו, וְצִוָּנוּ עַל נְטִילַת יָדָיִם:

One should not speak until after making the following two blessings and eating the matzah.

℠ מוֹצִיא ℞

The matzot are taken in the order that they are placed on the tray—
the broken piece between the two whole matzot—and the following blessing is recited.

בָּרוּךְ אַתָּה יְיָ, אֱלֹהֵינוּ מֶלֶךְ הָעוֹלָם, הַמּוֹצִיא לֶחֶם מִן הָאָרֶץ:

℠ מַצָּה ℞

After putting down the bottom matzah, the following blessing is recited over the broken matzah and the top one. This blessing also refers to the eating of the *Korech* and the eating of the *Afikoman*:

בָּרוּךְ אַתָּה יְיָ, אֱלֹהֵינוּ מֶלֶךְ הָעוֹלָם, אֲשֶׁר קִדְּשָׁנוּ בְּמִצְוֹתָיו וְצִוָּנוּ עַל אֲכִילַת מַצָּה:

All participants eat from both matzot in a reclining position.

℠ מָרוֹר ℞

The *maror* (bitter herbs) "the size of an olive" is dipped in *charoset* and eaten after reciting the following blessing:

בָּרוּךְ אַתָּה יְיָ, אֱלֹהֵינוּ מֶלֶךְ הָעוֹלָם, אֲשֶׁר קִדְּשָׁנוּ בְּמִצְוֹתָיו וְצִוָּנוּ עַל אֲכִילַת מָרוֹר:

ஒ   Rachtzah   ௸

The participants wash their hands and then recite the following blessing:

Blessed are You, Lord our God, King of the universe, who has sanctified us with His commandments and commanded us concerning the washing of the hands.

One should not speak until after making the following two blessings and eating the matzah.

ஒ   Motzi   ௸

The matzot are taken in the order that they are placed on the tray—
the broken piece between the two whole matzot—and the following blessing is recited.

Blessed are You, Lord our God, King of the universe, who brings forth bread from the earth.

ஒ   Matzah   ௸

After putting down the bottom matzah, the following blessing is recited over the broken matzah and the top one. This blessing also refers to the eating of the *Korech* and the eating of the *Afikoman*:

Blessed are You, Lord our God, King of the universe, who has sanctified us with His commandments and commanded us concerning the eating of matzah.

All participants eat from both matzot in a reclining position.

ஒ   Maror   ௸

The *maror* (bitter herbs) "the size of an olive" is dipped in *charoset*
and eaten after reciting the following blessing:

Blessed are You, Lord our God, King of the universe, who has sanctified us with His commandments and commanded us concerning the eating of maror.

‏& co‏ ‏כּוֹרֵךְ‏ ‏&‏

Maror is dipped in *charoset* and placed between two pieces of the bottom matzah. It is eaten as a "sandwich" in a reclining position following the recitation of the following:

זֵכֶר לְמִקְדָּשׁ כְּהִלֵּל: כֵּן עָשָׂה הִלֵּל בִּזְמַן שֶׁבֵּית הַמִּקְדָּשׁ הָיָה קַיָּם. הָיָה כּוֹרֵךְ פֶּסַח מַצָּה וּמָרוֹר וְאוֹכֵל בְּיַחַד. לְקַיֵּם מַה שֶּׁנֶּאֱמַר: עַל־מַצּוֹת וּמְרוֹרִים יֹאכְלֻהוּ:

‏&‏ ‏שֻׁלְחָן עוֹרֵךְ‏ ‏&co‏

The festive meal is eaten. It is a custom to eat a hard-boiled egg at the beginning of the meal. No roasted meat should be eaten, for this might be mistaken for the Pesach sacrifice, which is forbidden to be offered in exile. One should try to recline throughout the meal.

‏&‏ ‏צָפוּן‏ ‏&co‏

After the meal, the *Afikoman* is divided among all of the participants to be eaten in a reclining position. The *Afikoman* should be eaten before the midpoint of the night. No food or drink, other than the last two cups of wine, should be consumed after the eating of the *Afikoman*.

‏&‏ ‏בָּרֵךְ‏ ‏&co‏

שִׁיר הַמַּעֲלוֹת בְּשׁוּב יְיָ אֶת שִׁיבַת צִיּוֹן הָיִינוּ כְּחֹלְמִים: אָז יִמָּלֵא שְׂחוֹק פִּינוּ וּלְשׁוֹנֵנוּ רִנָּה אָז יֹאמְרוּ בַגּוֹיִם הִגְדִּיל יְיָ לַעֲשׂוֹת עִם אֵלֶּה: הִגְדִּיל יְיָ לַעֲשׂוֹת עִמָּנוּ הָיִינוּ שְׂמֵחִים: שׁוּבָה יְיָ אֶת שְׁבִיתֵנוּ כַּאֲפִיקִים בַּנֶּגֶב: הַזֹּרְעִים בְּדִמְעָה בְּרִנָּה יִקְצֹרוּ: הָלוֹךְ יֵלֵךְ וּבָכֹה נֹשֵׂא מֶשֶׁךְ הַזָּרַע בֹּא יָבֹא בְרִנָּה נֹשֵׂא אֲלֻמֹּתָיו:

℘ *Korekh* ℘

Maror is dipped in *charoset* and placed between two pieces of the bottom matzah. It is eaten as a "sandwich" in a reclining position following the recitation of the following:

In remembrance *of the Temple, we do as Hillel did at the time when the Temple was standing. He would combine matzah and maror in a sandwich and eat them together, to fulfill what is written in the Torah, "with matzot and bitter herbs shall they eat it."*

℘ *Shulchan Orekh* ℘

The festive meal is eaten. It is a custom to eat a hard-boiled egg at the beginning of the meal. No roasted meat should be eaten, for this might be mistaken for the Pesach sacrifice, which is forbidden to be offered in exile. One should try to recline throughout the meal.

℘ *Tzafun* ℘

After the meal, the *Afikoman* is divided among all of the participants to be eaten in a reclining position. The *Afikoman* should be eaten before the midpoint of the night. No food or drink, other than the last two cups of wine, should be consumed after the eating of the *Afikoman*.

℘ *Barekh* ℘

A song of Ascents. *When the Lord returns the captives of Zion, we will be like dreamers. Then our mouth will be filled with laughter, and our tongue with joyous song. Then will they say among the nations, "The Lord has done great things for these." The Lord has done great things for us, we were joyful. Lord, return our captivity like water-springs in the southern desert. Those who sow with tears will reap with great joy. Though he goes on his way weeping as he carries the seeds through the field, he will return singing, bearing his sheaves.*

When *Birkat Hamazon* is said with a quorum of three or more, the leader begins here.
With a quorum of ten or more, the words in parentheses are added:

המזמן: רַבּוֹתַי נְבָרֵךְ!

המסובין: יְהִי שֵׁם יְיָ מְבֹרָךְ מֵעַתָּה וְעַד עוֹלָם.

המזמן: יְהִי שֵׁם יְיָ מְבֹרָךְ מֵעַתָּה וְעַד עוֹלָם.
בִּרְשׁוּת מָרָנָן וְרַבָּנָן וְרַבּוֹתַי,
נְבָרֵךְ (אֱלֹהֵינוּ) שֶׁאָכַלְנוּ מִשֶּׁלּוֹ.

המסובין: בָּרוּךְ (אֱלֹהֵינוּ) שֶׁאָכַלְנוּ מִשֶּׁלּוֹ וּבְטוּבוֹ חָיִינוּ.

המזמן: בָּרוּךְ (אֱלֹהֵינוּ) שֶׁאָכַלְנוּ מִשֶּׁלּוֹ וּבְטוּבוֹ חָיִינוּ.

בָּרוּךְ הוּא וּבָרוּךְ שְׁמוֹ:

If there is no quorum, the *Birkat Hamazon* begins here:

בָּרוּךְ אַתָּה יְיָ, אֱלֹהֵינוּ מֶלֶךְ הָעוֹלָם, הַזָּן אֶת הָעוֹלָם כֻּלּוֹ בְּטוּבוֹ בְּחֵן בְּחֶסֶד וּבְרַחֲמִים הוּא נוֹתֵן לֶחֶם לְכָל בָּשָׂר כִּי לְעוֹלָם חַסְדּוֹ. וּבְטוּבוֹ הַגָּדוֹל תָּמִיד לֹא חָסַר לָנוּ, וְאַל יֶחְסַר לָנוּ מָזוֹן לְעוֹלָם וָעֶד. בַּעֲבוּר שְׁמוֹ הַגָּדוֹל, כִּי הוּא אֵל זָן וּמְפַרְנֵס לַכֹּל וּמֵטִיב לַכֹּל, וּמֵכִין מָזוֹן לְכָל בְּרִיּוֹתָיו אֲשֶׁר בָּרָא. בָּרוּךְ אַתָּה יְיָ, הַזָּן אֶת הַכֹּל:

נוֹדֶה לְךָ יְיָ אֱלֹהֵינוּ עַל שֶׁהִנְחַלְתָּ לַאֲבוֹתֵינוּ, אֶרֶץ חֶמְדָּה טוֹבָה וּרְחָבָה, וְעַל שֶׁהוֹצֵאתָנוּ יְיָ אֱלֹהֵינוּ מֵאֶרֶץ מִצְרַיִם, וּפְדִיתָנוּ, מִבֵּית עֲבָדִים, וְעַל בְּרִיתְךָ שֶׁחָתַמְתָּ בִּבְשָׂרֵנוּ, וְעַל תּוֹרָתְךָ שֶׁלִּמַּדְתָּנוּ, וְעַל חֻקֶּיךָ שֶׁהוֹדַעְתָּנוּ וְעַל חַיִּים חֵן וָחֶסֶד שֶׁחוֹנַנְתָּנוּ, וְעַל אֲכִילַת מָזוֹן שָׁאַתָּה זָן וּמְפַרְנֵס אוֹתָנוּ תָּמִיד, בְּכָל יוֹם וּבְכָל עֵת וּבְכָל שָׁעָה:

When *Birkat Hamazon* is said with a quorum of three or more, the leader begins here.
With a quorum of ten or more, the words in parentheses are added:

LEADER: *Gentlemen, let us say Grace!*

OTHERS: *May the Name of the Lord be blessed from now and forever.*

LEADER: *Blessed be the name of the Lord from now and forever. With the permission of the masters, teachers and gentlemen, let us bless (our God), from whose abundance we have eaten.*

OTHERS: *Blessed is (our God), from whose abundance we have eaten and through whose goodness we live.*

LEADER: *Blessed is (our God), from whose abundance we have eaten and through whose goodness we live.*

Blessed is He and blessed is His Name.

If there is no quorum, the *Birkat Hamazon* begins here:

Blessed are You, *Lord our God, King of the universe, who, in His goodness, nourishes the whole world with grace, with kindness, and with compassion. He gives nourishment to all flesh, for His kindness is eternal. And through His great goodness we have never lacked, and may we never lack food forever—for the sake of His great Name. For He is a God who provides and sustains all, does good to all, and prepares food for all His creatures whom He has created. Blessed are You, Lord, who provides food for all.*

We thank You, *Lord our God, for having given as an inheritance to our fathers a desirable, good and spacious land; for having brought us out, Lord our God, from the land of Egypt and redeemed us from the house of slavery; for Your covenant which You have sealed in our flesh; for Your Torah which You have taught us; for Your statutes which You have made known to us; for the life, favor and kindness which You have graciously bestowed upon us; and for the food which You provide for us and sustain us with constantly, in every day, in every season, and in every hour.*

וְעַל הַכֹּל יְיָ אֱלֹהֵינוּ אֲנַחְנוּ מוֹדִים לָךְ, וּמְבָרְכִים
אוֹתָךְ, יִתְבָּרַךְ שִׁמְךָ בְּפִי כָּל חַי תָּמִיד
לְעוֹלָם וָעֶד. כַּכָּתוּב, וְאָכַלְתָּ וְשָׂבָעְתָּ, וּבֵרַכְתָּ אֶת יְיָ אֱלֹהֶיךָ
עַל הָאָרֶץ הַטֹּבָה אֲשֶׁר נָתַן לָךְ. בָּרוּךְ אַתָּה יְיָ, עַל הָאָרֶץ וְעַל
הַמָּזוֹן:

רַחֶם נָא יְיָ אֱלֹהֵינוּ, עַל יִשְׂרָאֵל עַמֶּךָ, וְעַל יְרוּשָׁלַיִם
עִירֶךָ, וְעַל צִיּוֹן מִשְׁכַּן כְּבוֹדֶךָ, וְעַל מַלְכוּת
בֵּית דָּוִד מְשִׁיחֶךָ, וְעַל הַבַּיִת הַגָּדוֹל וְהַקָּדוֹשׁ שֶׁנִּקְרָא שִׁמְךָ
עָלָיו. אֱלֹהֵינוּ, אָבִינוּ, רְעֵנוּ, זוּנֵנוּ, פַּרְנְסֵנוּ, וְכַלְכְּלֵנוּ,
וְהַרְוִיחֵנוּ, וְהַרְוַח לָנוּ יְיָ אֱלֹהֵינוּ מְהֵרָה מִכָּל צָרוֹתֵינוּ, וְנָא, אַל
תַּצְרִיכֵנוּ יְיָ אֱלֹהֵינוּ, לֹא לִידֵי מַתְּנַת בָּשָׂר וָדָם, וְלֹא לִידֵי
הַלְוָאָתָם. כִּי אִם לְיָדְךָ הַמְּלֵאָה, הַפְּתוּחָה, הַקְּדוֹשָׁה וְהָרְחָבָה,
שֶׁלֹּא נֵבוֹשׁ וְלֹא נִכָּלֵם לְעוֹלָם וָעֶד:

The following paragraph is included on Shabbat:

רְצֵה וְהַחֲלִיצֵנוּ יְיָ אֱלֹהֵינוּ בְּמִצְוֹתֶיךָ וּבְמִצְוַת יוֹם הַשְּׁבִיעִי
הַשַּׁבָּת הַגָּדוֹל וְהַקָּדוֹשׁ הַזֶּה. כִּי יוֹם זֶה גָּדוֹל וְקָדוֹשׁ הוּא
לְפָנֶיךָ, לִשְׁבָּת בּוֹ וְלָנוּחַ בּוֹ בְּאַהֲבָה כְּמִצְוַת רְצוֹנֶךָ וּבִרְצוֹנְךָ הָנִיחַ לָנוּ
יְיָ אֱלֹהֵינוּ, שֶׁלֹּא תְהֵא צָרָה וְיָגוֹן וַאֲנָחָה בְּיוֹם מְנוּחָתֵנוּ. וְהַרְאֵנוּ יְיָ
אֱלֹהֵינוּ בְּנֶחָמַת צִיּוֹן עִירֶךָ, וּבְבִנְיַן יְרוּשָׁלַיִם עִיר קָדְשֶׁךָ, כִּי אַתָּה הוּא
בַּעַל הַיְשׁוּעוֹת וּבַעַל הַנֶּחָמוֹת:

For all this, *Lord our God, we thank You and bless You. May Your Name be blessed by the mouth of every living being, constantly and forever. As it is written: "When you have eaten and are satiated, you shall bless the Lord your God, for the good land which He has given you." Blessed are You, Lord, for the land and for the food.*

Have mercy, *Lord our God, upon Israel Your people, upon Jerusalem Your city, upon Zion the abode of Your glory, upon the kingship of the house of David, Your anointed; and upon the great and holy House upon which Your Name is called. Our God, our Father, our Shepherd, tend us, provide for us, sustain us, support us, and speedily grant us, Lord our God, relief from all our troubles. Lord our God, please do not make us dependent upon the gifts of mortal men nor upon their loans, but only upon Your full, open, holy and generous hand, that we may not be shamed or disgraced forever and ever.*

The following paragraph is included on Shabbat:

May it please You, *God, our Lord, to give us rest, through Your commandments and through the commandment of the seventh day, this great and holy Shabbat. For this day is great and holy before You, to refrain from work on it and to rest on it with love, in accordance with Your will. May it be Your will, God our Lord, to grant us rest, that there shall be no distress, grief or moaning on this day of our rest. And show us God our Lord, the consolation of Zion Your city, and the rebuilding of Jerusalem Your holy city, for You are the Master of salvation and the Master of consolation.*

אֱלֹהֵינוּ וֵאלֹהֵי אֲבוֹתֵינוּ, יַעֲלֶה וְיָבֹא וְיַגִּיעַ, וְיֵרָאֶה, וְיֵרָצֶה, וְיִשָּׁמַע, וְיִפָּקֵד, וְיִזָּכֵר זִכְרוֹנֵנוּ וּפִקְדוֹנֵנוּ, וְזִכְרוֹן אֲבוֹתֵינוּ, וְזִכְרוֹן מָשִׁיחַ בֶּן דָּוִד עַבְדֶּךָ, וְזִכְרוֹן יְרוּשָׁלַיִם עִיר קָדְשֶׁךָ, וְזִכְרוֹן כָּל עַמְּךָ בֵּית יִשְׂרָאֵל לְפָנֶיךָ, לִפְלֵיטָה לְטוֹבָה לְחֵן וּלְחֶסֶד וּלְרַחֲמִים, לְחַיִּים וּלְשָׁלוֹם בְּיוֹם חַג הַמַּצּוֹת הַזֶּה. זָכְרֵנוּ יְיָ אֱלֹהֵינוּ בּוֹ לְטוֹבָה. וּפָקְדֵנוּ בוֹ לִבְרָכָה. וְהוֹשִׁיעֵנוּ בוֹ לְחַיִּים, וּבִדְבַר יְשׁוּעָה וְרַחֲמִים, חוּס וְחָנֵּנוּ, וְרַחֵם עָלֵינוּ וְהוֹשִׁיעֵנוּ, כִּי אֵלֶיךָ עֵינֵינוּ, כִּי אֵל מֶלֶךְ חַנּוּן וְרַחוּם אָתָּה:

וּבְנֵה יְרוּשָׁלַיִם עִיר הַקֹּדֶשׁ בִּמְהֵרָה בְיָמֵינוּ. בָּרוּךְ אַתָּה יְיָ, בּוֹנֵה בְרַחֲמָיו יְרוּשָׁלָיִם. אָמֵן.

בָּרוּךְ אַתָּה יְיָ אֱלֹהֵינוּ מֶלֶךְ הָעוֹלָם, הָאֵל אָבִינוּ, מַלְכֵּנוּ, אַדִּירֵנוּ בּוֹרְאֵנוּ, גּוֹאֲלֵנוּ, יוֹצְרֵנוּ, קְדוֹשֵׁנוּ קְדוֹשׁ יַעֲקֹב, רוֹעֵנוּ רוֹעֵה יִשְׂרָאֵל. הַמֶּלֶךְ הַטּוֹב, וְהַמֵּטִיב לַכֹּל, שֶׁבְּכָל יוֹם וָיוֹם הוּא הֵטִיב, הוּא מֵטִיב, הוּא יֵיטִיב לָנוּ. הוּא גְמָלָנוּ, הוּא גוֹמְלֵנוּ, הוּא יִגְמְלֵנוּ לָעַד לְחֵן וּלְחֶסֶד וּלְרַחֲמִים וּלְרֶוַח הַצָּלָה וְהַצְלָחָה בְּרָכָה וִישׁוּעָה, נֶחָמָה, פַּרְנָסָה וְכַלְכָּלָה, וְרַחֲמִים, וְחַיִּים וְשָׁלוֹם, וְכָל טוֹב, וּמִכָּל טוּב לְעוֹלָם אַל יְחַסְּרֵנוּ:

Our God and God of our fathers, *may the remembrance and consideration of us; the remembrance of our fathers; the remembrance of Mashiach; son of David, Your servant; the remembrance of Jerusalem, the city of your holiness; the remembrance of all your people, the House of Israel, ascend, come and reach, be seen and accepted, heard, and be considered, and be remembered before You, for deliverance, for goodness, for grace, for kindness, for compassion, for life, and for peace, on this day of the Festival of Matzot. Remember us, Lord our God, on this day for goodness, consider us on it for blessing; and save us on it for life. And with Your word of salvation and mercy, pity us and be gracious and compassionate with us, and save us, for our eyes are turned to You, because You are a gracious and compassionate God and King.*

Rebuild Jerusalem, *the holy city, speedily in our days. Blessed are You, Lord, Who in His mercy rebuilds Jerusalem. Amen.*

Blessed are You, *Lord our God, King of the Universe, God our Father, our King, our Sovereign, our Creator, our Redeemer, our Maker, our Holy One, the Holy One of Yaakov, our Shepherd, the Shepherd of Israel, the King Who is good and Who continually does good to all, each and every day. He has done good for us, He does good for us, and He will do good for us; He was bountiful to us, He is bountiful to us, and He will be bountiful to us forever, with grace, kindness and with mercy, and with relief, salvation and success, blessing and help, consolation, sustenance and support, and with compassion and life and peace, and all goodness; and may He never deprive us of all good things.*

הָרַחֲמָן, הוּא יִמְלוֹךְ עָלֵינוּ לְעוֹלָם וָעֶד. הָרַחֲמָן, הוּא יִתְבָּרַךְ בַּשָּׁמַיִם וּבָאָרֶץ. הָרַחֲמָן, הוּא יִשְׁתַּבַּח לְדוֹר דּוֹרִים, וְיִתְפָּאַר בָּנוּ לָעַד וּלְנֵצַח נְצָחִים, וְיִתְהַדַּר בָּנוּ לָעַד וּלְעוֹלְמֵי עוֹלָמִים. הָרַחֲמָן, הוּא יְפַרְנְסֵנוּ בְּכָבוֹד. הָרַחֲמָן, הוּא יִשְׁבּוֹר עֻלֵּנוּ מֵעַל צַוָּארֵנוּ וְהוּא יוֹלִיכֵנוּ קוֹמְמִיּוּת לְאַרְצֵנוּ. הָרַחֲמָן, הוּא יִשְׁלַח לָנוּ בְּרָכָה מְרֻבָּה בַּבַּיִת הַזֶּה, וְעַל שֻׁלְחָן זֶה שֶׁאָכַלְנוּ עָלָיו. הָרַחֲמָן, הוּא יִשְׁלַח לָנוּ אֶת אֵלִיָּהוּ הַנָּבִיא זָכוּר לַטּוֹב, וִיבַשֶּׂר לָנוּ בְּשׂוֹרוֹת טוֹבוֹת יְשׁוּעוֹת וְנֶחָמוֹת.

הָרַחֲמָן, הוּא יְבָרֵךְ אֶת (אָבִי מוֹרִי) בַּעַל הַבַּיִת הַזֶּה, וְאֶת (אִמִּי מוֹרָתִי) בַּעֲלַת הַבַּיִת הַזֶּה, אוֹתָם וְאֶת בֵּיתָם וְאֶת זַרְעָם וְאֶת כָּל אֲשֶׁר לָהֶם.

הָרַחֲמָן, הוּא יְבָרֵךְ אוֹתִי (וְאָבִי וְאִמִּי וְאִשְׁתִּי וְזַרְעִי וְאֶת כָּל אֲשֶׁר לִי)

אוֹתָנוּ וְאֶת כָּל אֲשֶׁר לָנוּ, כְּמוֹ שֶׁנִּתְבָּרְכוּ אֲבוֹתֵינוּ, אַבְרָהָם יִצְחָק וְיַעֲקֹב: בַּכֹּל, מִכֹּל, כֹּל. כֵּן יְבָרֵךְ אוֹתָנוּ כֻּלָּנוּ יַחַד. בִּבְרָכָה שְׁלֵמָה, וְנֹאמַר אָמֵן:

בַּמָּרוֹם יְלַמְּדוּ עֲלֵיהֶם וְעָלֵינוּ זְכוּת, שֶׁתְּהֵא לְמִשְׁמֶרֶת שָׁלוֹם, וְנִשָּׂא בְרָכָה מֵאֵת יְיָ וּצְדָקָה מֵאֱלֹהֵי יִשְׁעֵנוּ, וְנִמְצָא חֵן וְשֵׂכֶל טוֹב בְּעֵינֵי אֱלֹהִים וְאָדָם:

May the Merciful One *reign over us forever and ever. May the Merciful One be blessed in heaven and on earth. May the Merciful One be praised for all generations, and be glorified through us forever and all eternity, and be honored through us forever and ever. May the Merciful One sustain us in honor. May the Merciful One break the yoke of exile from our neck and may He lead us upright to our land. May the Merciful One send abundant blessing into this house and upon this table at which we have eaten. May the Merciful One send us Eliyahu the Prophet, and let him bring us good tidings, salvation and consolation.*

May He bless (my father and teacher) the master of this house, and (my mother and teacher) the mistress of this house—them, their household, their children, and all that is theirs.

May the Merciful One bless me, my wife [husband], and my children, and all that is mine.

May He bless us and all that is ours—just as our forefathers, Avraham, Yitzchak and Yaakov were blessed in everything, from everything, and with everything. So may He bless us all together with a perfect blessing, and let us say, Amen.

In heaven, *may their merit and our merit be invoked as a safeguarding of peace. May we receive blessing from the Lord, and righteousness from the God of our salvation, and may we find favor and understanding in the eyes of God and man.*

On Shabbat add:

הָרַחֲמָן, הוּא יַנְחִילֵנוּ יוֹם שֶׁכֻּלּוֹ שַׁבָּת וּמְנוּחָה לְחַיֵּי הָעוֹלָמִים.

הָרַחֲמָן, הוּא יַנְחִילֵנוּ יוֹם שֶׁכֻּלּוֹ טוֹב.

הָרַחֲמָן, הוּא יְזַכֵּנוּ לִימוֹת הַמָּשִׁיחַ וּלְחַיֵּי הָעוֹלָם הַבָּא.

מִגְדּוֹל יְשׁוּעוֹת מַלְכּוֹ, וְעֹשֶׂה חֶסֶד לִמְשִׁיחוֹ לְדָוִד וּלְזַרְעוֹ עַד עוֹלָם: עֹשֶׂה שָׁלוֹם בִּמְרוֹמָיו, הוּא יַעֲשֶׂה שָׁלוֹם, עָלֵינוּ וְעַל כָּל יִשְׂרָאֵל, וְאִמְרוּ אָמֵן:

יְראוּ אֶת יְיָ קְדֹשָׁיו, כִּי אֵין מַחְסוֹר לִירֵאָיו: כְּפִירִים רָשׁוּ וְרָעֵבוּ, וְדוֹרְשֵׁי יְיָ לֹא יַחְסְרוּ כָל טוֹב: הוֹדוּ לַייָ כִּי טוֹב, כִּי לְעוֹלָם חַסְדּוֹ: פּוֹתֵחַ אֶת יָדֶךָ, וּמַשְׂבִּיעַ לְכָל חַי רָצוֹן: בָּרוּךְ הַגֶּבֶר אֲשֶׁר יִבְטַח בַּייָ, וְהָיָה יְיָ מִבְטַחוֹ: נַעַר הָיִיתִי גַם זָקַנְתִּי וְלֹא רָאִיתִי צַדִּיק נֶעֱזָב, וְזַרְעוֹ מְבַקֶּשׁ לָחֶם: יְיָ עֹז לְעַמּוֹ יִתֵּן, יְיָ יְבָרֵךְ אֶת עַמּוֹ בַשָּׁלוֹם:

The blessing over wine is recited and then the third cup is drunk while reclining on the left side.

בָּרוּךְ אַתָּה יְיָ, אֱלֹהֵינוּ מֶלֶךְ הָעוֹלָם, בּוֹרֵא פְּרִי הַגָּפֶן:

On Shabbat add:

May the Merciful One cause us to inherit the day which will be completely Shabbat and rest for eternal life.

May the Merciful One cause us to inherit the day which is all good.

May the Merciful One grant us the privilege of reaching the days of the Mashiach and the life of the World to Come.

He is a tower *of salvation to His king, and bestows kindness upon His anointed, to David and his descendants forever. He who makes peace in His heights, may He make peace for us and for all Israel; and say, Amen.*

Revere the Lord, *you His holy ones, for those who revere Him lack nothing. Young lions are in need and go hungry, but those who seek the Lord shall not lack any good. Give thanks to the Lord for He is good, for His kindness is everlasting. You open Your hand and satisfy the desire of every living thing. Blessed is the man who trusts in the Lord, and the Lord will be his trust. I was a youth and also have aged, and I have not seen a righteous man forsaken and his children begging for bread. God will give strength to His people, God will bless His people with peace.*

The blessing over wine is recited and then the third cup is drunk while reclining on the left side.

Blessed are You, Lord our God, King of the universe, Who creates the fruit of the vine.

We pour a cup in honor of the prophet Eliyahu. It is usually poured by the leader of the Seder.
While the Cup of Eliyahu is on the table, the door is opened for the prophet Eliyahu.
Everyone rises and says the following paragraph:

שְׁפֹךְ חֲמָתְךָ אֶל־הַגּוֹיִם, אֲשֶׁר לֹא יְדָעוּךָ וְעַל־מַמְלָכוֹת אֲשֶׁר בְּשִׁמְךָ לֹא קָרָאוּ: כִּי אָכַל אֶת־יַעֲקֹב. וְאֶת־נָוֵהוּ הֵשַׁמּוּ: שְׁפָךְ־עֲלֵיהֶם זַעְמֶךָ, וַחֲרוֹן אַפְּךָ יַשִּׂיגֵם: תִּרְדֹּף בְּאַף וְתַשְׁמִידֵם, מִתַּחַת שְׁמֵי יְיָ:

ﺑ הַלֵּל ﺑ

לֹא לָנוּ יְיָ לֹא לָנוּ כִּי לְשִׁמְךָ תֵּן כָּבוֹד, עַל חַסְדְּךָ עַל אֲמִתֶּךָ. לָמָּה יֹאמְרוּ הַגּוֹיִם, אַיֵּה נָא אֱלֹהֵיהֶם. וֵאלֹהֵינוּ בַשָּׁמָיִם כֹּל אֲשֶׁר חָפֵץ עָשָׂה. עֲצַבֵּיהֶם כֶּסֶף וְזָהָב, מַעֲשֵׂה יְדֵי אָדָם. פֶּה לָהֶם וְלֹא יְדַבֵּרוּ, עֵינַיִם לָהֶם וְלֹא יִרְאוּ. אָזְנַיִם לָהֶם וְלֹא יִשְׁמָעוּ, אַף לָהֶם וְלֹא יְרִיחוּן. יְדֵיהֶם וְלֹא יְמִישׁוּן, רַגְלֵיהֶם וְלֹא יְהַלֵּכוּ, לֹא יֶהְגּוּ בִּגְרוֹנָם. כְּמוֹהֶם יִהְיוּ עֹשֵׂיהֶם, כֹּל אֲשֶׁר בֹּטֵחַ בָּהֶם: יִשְׂרָאֵל בְּטַח בַּיְיָ, עֶזְרָם וּמָגִנָּם הוּא. בֵּית אַהֲרֹן בִּטְחוּ בַיְיָ, עֶזְרָם וּמָגִנָּם הוּא. יִרְאֵי יְיָ בִּטְחוּ בַיְיָ, עֶזְרָם וּמָגִנָּם הוּא:

יְיָ זְכָרָנוּ יְבָרֵךְ, יְבָרֵךְ אֶת בֵּית יִשְׂרָאֵל, יְבָרֵךְ אֶת בֵּית אַהֲרֹן. יְבָרֵךְ יִרְאֵי יְיָ, הַקְּטַנִּים עִם הַגְּדֹלִים. יֹסֵף יְיָ עֲלֵיכֶם, עֲלֵיכֶם וְעַל בְּנֵיכֶם. בְּרוּכִים אַתֶּם לַיְיָ, עֹשֵׂה שָׁמַיִם וָאָרֶץ. הַשָּׁמַיִם שָׁמַיִם לַיְיָ, וְהָאָרֶץ נָתַן לִבְנֵי אָדָם. לֹא הַמֵּתִים יְהַלְלוּ יָהּ, וְלֹא כָּל יֹרְדֵי דוּמָה. וַאֲנַחְנוּ נְבָרֵךְ יָהּ, מֵעַתָּה וְעַד עוֹלָם, הַלְלוּיָהּ:

We pour a cup in honor of the prophet Eliyahu. It is usually poured by the leader of the Seder.
While the Cup of Eliyahu is on the table, the door is opened for the prophet Eliyahu.
Everyone rises and says the following paragraph:

Pour out *Your wrath upon the nations that do not acknowledge You and upon the kingdoms that do not cry out Your Name (Tehillim 79:6–7). For they have devoured Yaakov and destroyed his habitation (Tehillim 69:55). Pour out Your anger upon them, and let Your wrath overtake them. Pursue them with wrath and annihilate them from beneath the heavens of the Lord (Eichah 3:66).*

ജ Hallel ര

Not for us, Lord, not for us, *but for Your Name's sake give honor, for Your kindness and Your truth. Why should the nations say, "Where is their God?" Our God is in the heavens, whatever He wills, He does. Their idols are of silver and gold, the product of human hands. They have a mouth, but cannot speak; they have eyes, but cannot see. They have ears, but cannot hear; they have a nose, but cannot smell; their hands cannot feel; their feet cannot walk; they can make no sound with their throat. Let those who make them become like them, whoever trusts in them! Israel, trust in the Lord! He is their help and their shield. House of Aaron, trust in the Lord! He is their help and their shield. You who fear the Lord, trust in the Lord! He is their help and their shield.*

The Lord, who has been mindful of us, *will bless—He will bless the House of Israel; He will bless the House of Aaron; He will bless those who revere the Lord, the small with the great. May the Lord increase you, you and your children. Blessed are you to the Lord, Maker of heaven and earth. The heavens are the heavens of the Lord, but the earth, He has given to mankind. The dead cannot praise God, nor any who go down into the silence of the grave. But we will bless God, from now to eternity. Halleluyah.*

אָהַבְתִּי כִּי יִשְׁמַע יְיָ, אֶת קוֹלִי תַּחֲנוּנָי. כִּי הִטָּה אָזְנוֹ
לִי וּבְיָמַי אֶקְרָא: אֲפָפוּנִי חֶבְלֵי מָוֶת, וּמְצָרֵי
שְׁאוֹל מְצָאוּנִי צָרָה וְיָגוֹן אֶמְצָא. וּבְשֵׁם יְיָ אֶקְרָא, אָנָּה יְיָ
מַלְּטָה נַפְשִׁי. חַנּוּן יְיָ וְצַדִּיק, וֵאלֹהֵינוּ מְרַחֵם. שֹׁמֵר פְּתָאיִם יְיָ
דַּלּוֹתִי וְלִי יְהוֹשִׁיעַ. שׁוּבִי נַפְשִׁי לִמְנוּחָיְכִי, כִּי יְיָ גָּמַל עָלָיְכִי.
כִּי חִלַּצְתָּ נַפְשִׁי מִמָּוֶת אֶת עֵינִי מִן דִּמְעָה, אֶת רַגְלִי מִדֶּחִי.
אֶתְהַלֵּךְ לִפְנֵי יְיָ, בְּאַרְצוֹת הַחַיִּים. הֶאֱמַנְתִּי כִּי אֲדַבֵּר, אֲנִי
עָנִיתִי מְאֹד. אֲנִי אָמַרְתִּי בְחָפְזִי כָּל הָאָדָם כֹּזֵב.

מָה אָשִׁיב לַיְיָ, כָּל תַּגְמוּלוֹהִי עָלָי. כּוֹס יְשׁוּעוֹת
אֶשָּׂא, וּבְשֵׁם יְיָ אֶקְרָא. נְדָרַי לַיְיָ
אֲשַׁלֵּם, נֶגְדָה נָּא לְכָל עַמּוֹ. יָקָר בְּעֵינֵי יְיָ הַמָּוְתָה לַחֲסִידָיו.
אָנָּה יְיָ כִּי אֲנִי עַבְדֶּךָ אֲנִי עַבְדְּךָ, בֶּן אֲמָתֶךָ פִּתַּחְתָּ לְמוֹסֵרָי.
לְךָ אֶזְבַּח זֶבַח תּוֹדָה וּבְשֵׁם יְיָ אֶקְרָא. נְדָרַי לַיְיָ אֲשַׁלֵּם נֶגְדָה
נָּא לְכָל עַמּוֹ. בְּחַצְרוֹת בֵּית יְיָ בְּתוֹכֵכִי יְרוּשָׁלַיִם הַלְלוּיָהּ.

הַלְלוּ אֶת יְיָ, כָּל גּוֹיִם, שַׁבְּחוּהוּ כָּל הָאֻמִּים. כִּי גָבַר
עָלֵינוּ חַסְדּוֹ, וֶאֱמֶת יְיָ לְעוֹלָם הַלְלוּיָהּ:

כִּי לְעוֹלָם חַסְדּוֹ:	הוֹדוּ לַיְיָ כִּי טוֹב,
כִּי לְעוֹלָם חַסְדּוֹ:	יֹאמַר נָא יִשְׂרָאֵל,
כִּי לְעוֹלָם חַסְדּוֹ:	יֹאמְרוּ נָא בֵית אַהֲרֹן,
כִּי לְעוֹלָם חַסְדּוֹ:	יֹאמְרוּ נָא יִרְאֵי יְיָ,

I love it when the Lord hears my voice, my prayers. For He has inclined His ear to me; and in my own days I will call upon Him. The pains of death encompassed me, and the confines of the grave have found me, trouble and sorrow I encountered and I called upon the Name of the Lord: "Please, Lord, deliver my soul!" The Lord is gracious and just, our God is compassionate. The Lord watches over the simple; I was brought low, but He saved me. Return, my soul, to your resting place, for the Lord has dealt kindly with you. For You have delivered my soul from death, my eyes from tears, my feet from stumbling. I shall walk before the Lord in the land of the living. I had faith even while speaking of how I suffer so much [even though] I said in haste, "All mankind is deceitful."

How can I repay the Lord for all His kindnesses to me? I will raise the cup of salvation and call upon the Name of the Lord. I will pay my vows to the Lord in the presence of all His people. Precious in the eyes of the Lord is the death of His devout ones. Please, Lord, for I am Your servant, I am Your servant the son of Your handmaid: You have released my bonds. To You I will bring an offering of thanksgiving, and I will call upon the Name of the Lord. I will pay my vows to the Lord in the presence of all His people, in the courtyards of the House of the Lord, in the midst of Jerusalem. Halleluyah.

Praise the Lord, all nations! Extol Him, all peoples! For His kindness has overwhelmed us, and the truth of the Lord is everlasting. Halleluyah.

Give thanks to the Lord for He is good:	His kindness is everlasting.
Let Israel say:	His kindness is everlasting.
Let the House of Aaron say:	His kindness is everlasting.
Let those who revere the Lord say:	His kindness is everlasting.

מִן הַמֵּצַר קָרָאתִי יָּה, עָנָנִי בַמֶּרְחָב יָה. יְיָ לִי לֹא אִירָא, מַה יַּעֲשֶׂה לִי אָדָם. יְיָ לִי בְּעֹזְרָי, וַאֲנִי אֶרְאֶה בְשׂנְאָי. טוֹב לַחֲסוֹת בַּיְיָ, מִבְּטֹחַ בָּאָדָם. טוֹב לַחֲסוֹת בַּיְיָ מִבְּטֹחַ בִּנְדִיבִים. כָּל גּוֹיִם סְבָבוּנִי בְּשֵׁם יְיָ כִּי אֲמִילַם. סַבּוּנִי גַם סְבָבוּנִי בְּשֵׁם יְיָ כִּי אֲמִילַם. סַבּוּנִי כִדְבֹרִים דֹּעֲכוּ כְּאֵשׁ קוֹצִים, בְּשֵׁם יְיָ כִּי אֲמִילַם. דָּחֹה דְחִיתַנִי לִנְפֹּל, וַיְיָ עֲזָרָנִי. עָזִּי וְזִמְרָת יָה, וַיְהִי לִי לִישׁוּעָה. קוֹל רִנָּה וִישׁוּעָה בְּאָהֳלֵי צַדִּיקִים, יְמִין יְיָ עֹשָׂה חָיִל. יְמִין יְיָ רוֹמֵמָה, יְמִין יְיָ עֹשָׂה חָיִל. לֹא אָמוּת כִּי אֶחְיֶה, וַאֲסַפֵּר מַעֲשֵׂי יָה. יַסֹּר יִסְּרַנִי יָּה, וְלַמָּוֶת לֹא נְתָנָנִי. פִּתְחוּ לִי שַׁעֲרֵי צֶדֶק, אָבֹא בָם אוֹדֶה יָּה. זֶה הַשַּׁעַר לַיְיָ, צַדִּיקִים יָבֹאוּ בוֹ. **אוֹדְךָ** כִּי עֲנִיתָנִי, וַתְּהִי לִי לִישׁוּעָה. **אוֹדְךָ** כִּי עֲנִיתָנִי וַתְּהִי לִי לִישׁוּעָה. **אֶבֶן** מָאֲסוּ הַבּוֹנִים, הָיְתָה לְרֹאשׁ פִּנָּה. **אֶבֶן** מָאֲסוּ הַבּוֹנִים, הָיְתָה לְרֹאשׁ פִּנָּה. **מֵאֵת** יְיָ הָיְתָה זֹּאת, הִיא נִפְלָאת בְּעֵינֵינוּ. **מֵאֵת** יְיָ הָיְתָה זֹּאת, הִיא נִפְלָאת בְּעֵינֵינוּ. **זֶה** הַיּוֹם עָשָׂה יְיָ, נָגִילָה וְנִשְׂמְחָה בוֹ. זֶה הַיּוֹם עָשָׂה יְיָ נָגִילָה וְנִשְׂמְחָה בוֹ.

אָנָּא יְיָ הוֹשִׁיעָה נָּא:	**אָנָּא** יְיָ הוֹשִׁיעָה נָּא:
אָנָּא יְיָ הַצְלִיחָה נָא:	**אָנָּא** יְיָ הַצְלִיחָה נָא:

Out of narrow confines *I called to God; God answered me with abundance.… The Lord is with me, I will not fear—what can man do to me? The Lord is with me, through my helpers, and I can face my enemies. It is better to rely on the Lord than to trust in man. It is better to rely on the Lord than to trust in nobles. All the nations surround me; in the Name of the Lord I cut them down! They encircle me like bees, but they are quenched like a fire of thorns; in the Name of the Lord I cut them down. You pushed me again and again that I might fall, but the Lord helped me. God is my strength and song, and He was for me, my salvation. The sound of joyous song and salvation is in the tents of the righteous: "The right hand of the Lord performs deeds of valor." The Lord's right hand is exalted; the right hand of the Lord performs deeds of valor! I shall not die, but I shall live and relate the deeds of God. God has chastised me, but He did not let me die. Open for me the gates of righteousness—I will enter them and thank God. This is the gate of the Lord, the righteous will enter it.* **I thank You** *for You have answered me, and You brought me salvation.* **I thank You,** *for You have answered me and become my salvation.* **The stone** *scorned by the builders has become the cornerstone.* **The stone** *scorned by the builders has become the cornerstone.* **This thing** *is from the Lord, it is wondrous in our eyes.* **This thing** *is from the Lord, it is wondrous in our eyes.* **This is the day** *that the Lord has made, let us be glad and rejoice on it.* **This is the day** *that the Lord has made, let us be glad and rejoice on it.*

O Lord, please save us!

O Lord, please grant us success!

O Lord, please save us!

O Lord, please grant us success!

בָּרוּךְ הַבָּא בְּשֵׁם יְיָ, בֵּרַכְנוּכֶם מִבֵּית יְיָ. בָּרוּךְ הַבָּא בְּשֵׁם
יְיָ, בֵּרַכְנוּכֶם מִבֵּית יְיָ. **אֵל** יְיָ וַיָּאֶר לָנוּ, אִסְרוּ חַג
בַּעֲבֹתִים עַד קַרְנוֹת הַמִּזְבֵּחַ. **אֵל** יְיָ וַיָּאֶר לָנוּ, אִסְרוּ חַג בַּעֲבֹתִים,
עַד קַרְנוֹת הַמִּזְבֵּחַ. **אֵלִי** אַתָּה וְאוֹדֶךָּ אֱלֹהַי אֲרוֹמְמֶךָּ. **אֵלִי** אַתָּה
וְאוֹדֶךָ אֱלֹהַי אֲרוֹמְמֶךָ: **הוֹדוּ** לַיְיָ כִּי טוֹב, כִּי לְעוֹלָם חַסְדּוֹ: הוֹדוּ
לַיְיָ כִּי טוֹב, כִּי לְעוֹלָם חַסְדּוֹ.

יְהַלְלוּךָ יְיָ אֱלֹהֵינוּ כָּל מַעֲשֶׂיךָ, וַחֲסִידֶיךָ צַדִּיקִים
עוֹשֵׂי רְצוֹנֶךָ, וְכָל עַמְּךָ בֵּית יִשְׂרָאֵל בְּרִנָּה
יוֹדוּ וִיבָרְכוּ וִישַׁבְּחוּ וִיפָאֲרוּ וִירוֹמְמוּ וְיַעֲרִיצוּ וְיַקְדִּישׁוּ וְיַמְלִיכוּ
אֶת שִׁמְךָ מַלְכֵּנוּ, כִּי לְךָ טוֹב לְהוֹדוֹת וּלְשִׁמְךָ נָאֶה לְזַמֵּר, כִּי
מֵעוֹלָם וְעַד עוֹלָם אַתָּה אֵל.

הוֹדוּ לַיְיָ כִּי טוֹב,	כִּי לְעוֹלָם חַסְדּוֹ:
הוֹדוּ לֵאלֹהֵי הָאֱלֹהִים,	כִּי לְעוֹלָם חַסְדּוֹ:
הוֹדוּ לַאֲדֹנֵי הָאֲדֹנִים,	כִּי לְעוֹלָם חַסְדּוֹ:
לְעֹשֵׂה נִפְלָאוֹת גְּדֹלוֹת לְבַדּוֹ,	כִּי לְעוֹלָם חַסְדּוֹ:
לְעֹשֵׂה הַשָּׁמַיִם בִּתְבוּנָה,	כִּי לְעוֹלָם חַסְדּוֹ:
לְרוֹקַע הָאָרֶץ עַל הַמָּיִם,	כִּי לְעוֹלָם חַסְדּוֹ:
לְעֹשֵׂה אוֹרִים גְּדֹלִים,	כִּי לְעוֹלָם חַסְדּוֹ:
אֶת הַשֶּׁמֶשׁ לְמֶמְשֶׁלֶת בַּיּוֹם,	כִּי לְעוֹלָם חַסְדּוֹ:
אֶת הַיָּרֵחַ וְכוֹכָבִים לְמֶמְשְׁלוֹת בַּלָּיְלָה,	כִּי לְעוֹלָם חַסְדּוֹ:

Blessed *is he who comes in the Name of the Lord; we bless you from the House of the Lord.* **Blessed** *is he who comes in the Name of the Lord; we bless you from the House of the Lord.* **The Lord is Almighty,** *He gave us light; bring the festival offering, bound with cords to the corners of the altar.* **The Lord is Almighty,** *He gave us light; bring the festival offering, bound with cords to the corners of the altar.* **You are my God** *and I will thank You; my God and I will exalt You.* **You are my God** *and I will thank You; my God and I will exalt You.* **Give thanks** *to the Lord, for He is good; His kindness is everlasting.* **Give thanks** *to the Lord, for He is good; His kindness is everlasting.*

Lord our God, *all Your creations shall praise You; Your devout ones, the righteous who do Your will, and Your entire nation the House of Israel, with joyous song will thank and bless, laud and glorify, exalt and adore, sanctify and proclaim the sovereignty of Your Name, our King. For it is good to thank You, and befitting to sing to Your Name, for in this world and for eternity You are Almighty God.*

Give thanks to the Lord, for He is good	*for His kindness is everlasting.*
Give thanks to the God of Gods	*for His kindness is everlasting.*
Give thanks to the Master of Masters	*for His kindness is everlasting.*
To Him who alone does great wonders	*for His kindness is everlasting.*
To Him who made the heavens with understanding	*for His kindness is everlasting.*
To Him who spread out the earth upon the waters	*for His kindness is everlasting.*
To Him who made great lights	*for His kindness is everlasting.*
The sun, to rule by day	*for His kindness is everlasting.*
The moon and stars, to rule by night	*for His kindness is everlasting.*

כִּי לְעוֹלָם חַסְדּוֹ:	לְמַכֵּה מִצְרַיִם בִּבְכוֹרֵיהֶם,
כִּי לְעוֹלָם חַסְדּוֹ:	וַיּוֹצֵא יִשְׂרָאֵל מִתּוֹכָם,
כִּי לְעוֹלָם חַסְדּוֹ:	בְּיָד חֲזָקָה וּבִזְרוֹעַ נְטוּיָה,
כִּי לְעוֹלָם חַסְדּוֹ:	לְגֹזֵר יַם סוּף לִגְזָרִים,
כִּי לְעוֹלָם חַסְדּוֹ:	וְהֶעֱבִיר יִשְׂרָאֵל בְּתוֹכוֹ,
כִּי לְעוֹלָם חַסְדּוֹ:	וְנִעֵר פַּרְעֹה וְחֵילוֹ בְיַם סוּף,
כִּי לְעוֹלָם חַסְדּוֹ:	לְמוֹלִיךְ עַמּוֹ בַּמִּדְבָּר,
כִּי לְעוֹלָם חַסְדּוֹ:	לְמַכֵּה מְלָכִים גְּדֹלִים,
כִּי לְעוֹלָם חַסְדּוֹ:	וַיַּהֲרֹג מְלָכִים אַדִּירִים,
כִּי לְעוֹלָם חַסְדּוֹ:	לְסִיחוֹן מֶלֶךְ הָאֱמֹרִי,
כִּי לְעוֹלָם חַסְדּוֹ:	וּלְעוֹג מֶלֶךְ הַבָּשָׁן,
כִּי לְעוֹלָם חַסְדּוֹ:	וְנָתַן אַרְצָם לְנַחֲלָה,
כִּי לְעוֹלָם חַסְדּוֹ:	נַחֲלָה לְיִשְׂרָאֵל עַבְדּוֹ,
כִּי לְעוֹלָם חַסְדּוֹ:	שֶׁבְּשִׁפְלֵנוּ זָכַר לָנוּ,
כִּי לְעוֹלָם חַסְדּוֹ:	וַיִּפְרְקֵנוּ מִצָּרֵינוּ,
כִּי לְעוֹלָם חַסְדּוֹ:	נוֹתֵן לֶחֶם לְכָל בָּשָׂר,
כִּי לְעוֹלָם חַסְדּוֹ:	הוֹדוּ לְאֵל הַשָּׁמַיִם,

נִשְׁמַת כָּל חַי, תְּבָרֵךְ אֶת שִׁמְךָ יְיָ אֱלֹהֵינוּ. וְרוּחַ כָּל בָּשָׂר, תְּפָאֵר וּתְרוֹמֵם זִכְרְךָ מַלְכֵּנוּ תָּמִיד, מִן הָעוֹלָם וְעַד הָעוֹלָם אַתָּה אֵל. וּמִבַּלְעָדֶיךָ אֵין לָנוּ מֶלֶךְ גּוֹאֵל וּמוֹשִׁיעַ, פּוֹדֶה וּמַצִּיל וּמְפַרְנֵס וּמְרַחֵם, בְּכָל עֵת צָרָה וְצוּקָה.

To Him who smote Egypt	
through their firstborn	*for His kindness is everlasting.*
And brought Israel out of their midst	*for His kindness is everlasting.*
With a strong hand	
and with an outstretched arm	*for His kindness is everlasting.*
To Him who split	
the Sea of Reeds into sections	*for His kindness is everlasting.*
And led Israel through it	*for His kindness is everlasting.*
And cast Pharaoh and his army	
into the Sea of Reeds	*for His kindness is everlasting.*
To Him who led His people	
through the wildnerness	*for His kindness is everlasting.*
To Him who smote great kings	*for His kindness is everlasting.*
And slew mighty kings	*for His kindness is everlasting.*
Sichon, king of the Amorites	*for His kindness is everlasting.*
And Og, king of Bashan	*for His kindness is everlasting.*
And gave us their land as an inheritance	*for His kindness is everlasting.*
An inheritance to Israel, His servant	*for His kindness is everlasting.*
Who remembered us in our lowliness	*for His kindness is everlasting.*
And delivered us from our oppressors	*for His kindness is everlasting.*
Who gives food to all flesh	*for His kindness is everlasting.*
Give thanks to the God of heavens	*for His kindness is everlasting.*

The soul *of every living being shall bless Your Name, Lord, our God; the spirit of all flesh shall always glorify and exalt Your remembrance, our King. In this world and for eternity You are God, and besides You we have no King, Redeemer and Savior who delivers, rescues, saves, sustains, and is merciful in every time of trouble and distress; we have no King but You. You are the God*

אֵין לָנוּ מֶלֶךְ אֶלָּא אַתָּה: אֱלֹהֵי הָרִאשׁוֹנִים וְהָאַחֲרוֹנִים, אֱלוֹהַּ כָּל בְּרִיּוֹת, אֲדוֹן כָּל תּוֹלָדוֹת, הַמְהֻלָּל בְּרֹב הַתִּשְׁבָּחוֹת, הַמְנַהֵג עוֹלָמוֹ בְּחֶסֶד, וּבְרִיּוֹתָיו בְּרַחֲמִים. וַיְיָ לֹא יָנוּם וְלֹא יִישָׁן, הַמְעוֹרֵר יְשֵׁנִים וְהַמֵּקִיץ נִרְדָּמִים, וְהַמֵּשִׂיחַ אִלְּמִים, וְהַמַּתִּיר אֲסוּרִים, וְהַסּוֹמֵךְ נוֹפְלִים, וְהַזּוֹקֵף כְּפוּפִים, לְךָ לְבַדְּךָ אֲנַחְנוּ מוֹדִים.

אִלּוּ פִּינוּ מָלֵא שִׁירָה כַּיָּם, וּלְשׁוֹנֵנוּ רִנָּה כַּהֲמוֹן גַּלָּיו, וְשִׂפְתוֹתֵינוּ שֶׁבַח כְּמֶרְחֲבֵי רָקִיעַ, וְעֵינֵינוּ מְאִירוֹת כַּשֶּׁמֶשׁ וְכַיָּרֵחַ, וְיָדֵינוּ פְרוּשׂוֹת כְּנִשְׁרֵי שָׁמָיִם, וְרַגְלֵינוּ קַלּוֹת כָּאַיָּלוֹת, אֵין אֲנַחְנוּ מַסְפִּיקִים, לְהוֹדוֹת לְךָ יְיָ אֱלֹהֵינוּ וֵאלֹהֵי אֲבוֹתֵינוּ, וּלְבָרֵךְ אֶת שְׁמֶךָ עַל אַחַת מֵאֶלֶף אֶלֶף אַלְפֵי אֲלָפִים וְרִבֵּי רְבָבוֹת פְּעָמִים, הַטּוֹבוֹת שֶׁעָשִׂיתָ עִם אֲבוֹתֵינוּ וְעִמָּנוּ. מִמִּצְרַיִם גְּאַלְתָּנוּ יְיָ אֱלֹהֵינוּ, וּמִבֵּית עֲבָדִים פְּדִיתָנוּ, בְּרָעָב זַנְתָּנוּ, וּבְשָׂבָע כִּלְכַּלְתָּנוּ, מֵחֶרֶב הִצַּלְתָּנוּ, וּמִדֶּבֶר מִלַּטְתָּנוּ, וּמֵחֳלָיִם רָעִים וְנֶאֱמָנִים דִּלִּיתָנוּ: עַד הֵנָּה עֲזָרוּנוּ רַחֲמֶיךָ, וְלֹא עֲזָבוּנוּ חֲסָדֶיךָ וְאַל תִּטְּשֵׁנוּ יְיָ אֱלֹהֵינוּ לָנֶצַח.

עַל כֵּן אֵבָרִים שֶׁפִּלַּגְתָּ בָּנוּ, וְרוּחַ וּנְשָׁמָה שֶׁנָּפַחְתָּ בְּאַפֵּינוּ, וְלָשׁוֹן אֲשֶׁר שַׂמְתָּ בְּפִינוּ, הֵן הֵם יוֹדוּ וִיבָרְכוּ וִישַׁבְּחוּ וִיפָאֲרוּ וִירוֹמְמוּ וְיַעֲרִיצוּ וְיַקְדִּישׁוּ וְיַמְלִיכוּ אֶת שִׁמְךָ מַלְכֵּנוּ, כִּי כָל פֶּה לְךָ יוֹדֶה, וְכָל לָשׁוֹן לְךָ תִשָּׁבַע, וְכָל בֶּרֶךְ לְךָ תִכְרַע, וְכָל קוֹמָה לְפָנֶיךָ תִשְׁתַּחֲוֶה, וְכָל לְבָבוֹת

of the first and of the last, God of all creatures, Lord of all generations, who is extolled with manifold praises, who directs His world with kindness and His creatures with compassion. Behold, the Lord neither slumbers nor sleeps. He arouses the sleepers and awakens the slumberous, gives speech to the mute, releases the bound, supports the falling and raises up those who are bowed. To You alone we give thanks.

Were *our mouths as full of song as the sea, and our tongues with joyous singing like the multitudes of its waves, and our lips with praise like the expanse of the sky; and our eyes shining like the sun and the moon, and our hands spread out like the eagles of heaven, and our feet swift like deer we would still be unable to thank You Lord, our God and God of our fathers, and to bless Your Name, for even one of the thousands, and myriads of favors which You have done for us and for our fathers before us. Lord our God. You have redeemed us from Egypt, You have freed us from the house of bondage, You have fed us in famine and nourished us in times of plenty; You have saved us from the sword and delivered us from pestilence, and rescued us from evil and lasting diseases. Until now Your mercies have helped us, and Your kindnesses have not forsaken us; and do not abandon us, Lord our God, forever!*

Therefore, *the limbs which You have formed for us, and the spirit and soul which You have breathed into our nostrils, and the tongue which You have placed in our mouth all shall thank, bless, praise, glorify, exalt, adore, sanctify and proclaim the sovereignty of Your Name, our King. For every mouth shall offer thanks to You, every tongue shall swear loyalty to You, every knee shall bend to You, all who stand erect shall bow down before You, all hearts shall*

יִירָאוּךָ, וְכָל קֶרֶב וּכְלָיוֹת יְזַמְּרוּ לִשְׁמֶךָ. כַּדָּבָר שֶׁכָּתוּב, כָּל עַצְמוֹתַי תֹּאמַרְנָה יְיָ מִי כָמוֹךָ. מַצִּיל עָנִי מֵחָזָק מִמֶּנּוּ, וְעָנִי וְאֶבְיוֹן מִגֹּזְלוֹ: מִי יִדְמֶה לָּךְ, וּמִי יִשְׁוֶה לָּךְ וּמִי יַעֲרָךְ לָךְ: הָאֵל הַגָּדוֹל הַגִּבּוֹר וְהַנּוֹרָא, אֵל עֶלְיוֹן קֹנֵה שָׁמַיִם וָאָרֶץ: נְהַלֶּלְךָ וּנְשַׁבֵּחֲךָ וּנְפָאֶרְךָ וּנְבָרֵךְ אֶת־שֵׁם קָדְשֶׁךָ. כָּאָמוּר, לְדָוִד, בָּרְכִי נַפְשִׁי אֶת יְיָ, וְכָל קְרָבַי אֶת שֵׁם קָדְשׁוֹ:

הָאֵל בְּתַעֲצֻמוֹת עֻזֶּךָ, הַגָּדוֹל בִּכְבוֹד שְׁמֶךָ. הַגִּבּוֹר לָנֶצַח וְהַנּוֹרָא בְּנוֹרְאוֹתֶיךָ. הַמֶּלֶךְ הַיּוֹשֵׁב עַל כִּסֵּא רָם וְנִשָּׂא:

שׁוֹכֵן עַד, מָרוֹם וְקָדוֹשׁ שְׁמוֹ: וְכָתוּב, רַנְּנוּ צַדִּיקִים בַּיְיָ, לַיְשָׁרִים נָאוָה תְהִלָּה. בְּפִי יְשָׁרִים תִּתְהַלָּל. וּבְדִבְרֵי צַדִּיקִים תִּתְבָּרַךְ. וּבִלְשׁוֹן חֲסִידִים תִּתְרוֹמָם. וּבְקֶרֶב קְדוֹשִׁים תִּתְקַדָּשׁ:

וּבְמַקְהֲלוֹת רִבְבוֹת עַמְּךָ בֵּית יִשְׂרָאֵל, בְּרִנָּה יִתְפָּאֵר שִׁמְךָ מַלְכֵּנוּ, בְּכָל דּוֹר וָדוֹר, שֶׁכֵּן חוֹבַת כָּל הַיְצוּרִים, לְפָנֶיךָ יְיָ אֱלֹהֵינוּ, וֵאלֹהֵי אֲבוֹתֵינוּ, לְהוֹדוֹת לְהַלֵּל לְשַׁבֵּחַ לְפָאֵר לְרוֹמֵם לְהַדֵּר לְבָרֵךְ לְעַלֵּה וּלְקַלֵּס, עַל כָּל דִּבְרֵי שִׁירוֹת וְתִשְׁבְּחוֹת דָּוִד בֶּן יִשַׁי עַבְדְּךָ מְשִׁיחֶךָ:

fear You, and every innermost part shall sing praise to Your Name, as it is written: "All my bones will say, Lord, who is like You; You save the poor from one stronger than he, the poor and the needy from one who would rob him!" Who can be likened to You, who is equal to You, who can be compared to You, the great, mighty, awesome God, God most high, Possessor of heaven and earth! We will laud You, praise You and glorify You, and we will bless Your holy Name, as it says: "A Psalm of David; bless the Lord, O my soul, and all that is within me bless His holy Name."

You are the Almighty God *in the power of Your strength; great in the glory of Your Name; mighty forever, and awe-inspiring in Your awesome deeds; the King who sits upon a lofty and exalted throne.*

He who dwells for eternity, *lofty and holy is His Name. And it is written: "Exult, righteous ones, before God; for the upright praise is fitting." By the mouth of the upright You are praised; by the word of the righteous You shall be blessed; by the tongue of the devout You shall be exalted; and among the holy ones You shall be sanctified.*

And in the assembled *multitudes of Your people, the House of Israel, with joyous song Your Name, our King, is glorified in every generation. For such is the obligation of all creatures before You, Lord our God and God of our fathers, to thank, to laud, to praise, to glorify, to exalt, to adore, to bless, to elevate and to honor You, even beyond all the words of songs and praises of David son of Yishai, Your anointed servant.*

יִשְׁתַּבַּח שִׁמְךָ לָעַד מַלְכֵּנוּ, הָאֵל הַמֶּלֶךְ הַגָּדוֹל וְהַקָּדוֹשׁ בַּשָּׁמַיִם וּבָאָרֶץ. כִּי לְךָ נָאֶה, יְיָ, אֱלֹהֵינוּ וֵאלֹהֵי אֲבוֹתֵינוּ: שִׁיר וּשְׁבָחָה, הַלֵּל וְזִמְרָה, עֹז וּמֶמְשָׁלָה, נֶצַח, גְּדֻלָּה וּגְבוּרָה, תְּהִלָּה וְתִפְאֶרֶת, קְדֻשָּׁה וּמַלְכוּת. בְּרָכוֹת וְהוֹדָאוֹת מֵעַתָּה וְעַד עוֹלָם. בָּרוּךְ אַתָּה יְיָ, אֵל מֶלֶךְ גָּדוֹל (וּמְהֻלָּל) בַּתִּשְׁבָּחוֹת, אֵל הַהוֹדָאוֹת, אֲדוֹן הַנִּפְלָאוֹת, הַבּוֹחֵר בְּשִׁירֵי זִמְרָה, מֶלֶךְ אֵל חֵי הָעוֹלָמִים.

The following blessing is recited before drinking the fourth cup in a reclining position:

בָּרוּךְ אַתָּה יְיָ, אֱלֹהֵינוּ מֶלֶךְ הָעוֹלָם, בּוֹרֵא פְּרִי הַגָּפֶן:

After drinking the fourth cup, the concluding blessing is recited.
On Shabbat, include the passage in parentheses:

בָּרוּךְ אַתָּה יְיָ אֱלֹהֵינוּ מֶלֶךְ הָעוֹלָם עַל הַגֶּפֶן וְעַל פְּרִי הַגָּפֶן.

וְעַל תְּנוּבַת הַשָּׂדֶה, וְעַל אֶרֶץ חֶמְדָּה טוֹבָה וּרְחָבָה, שֶׁרָצִיתָ וְהִנְחַלְתָּ לַאֲבוֹתֵינוּ, לֶאֱכוֹל מִפִּרְיָהּ וְלִשְׂבּוֹעַ מִטּוּבָהּ. רַחֶם נָא יְיָ אֱלֹהֵינוּ עַל יִשְׂרָאֵל עַמֶּךָ, וְעַל יְרוּשָׁלַיִם עִירֶךָ, וְעַל צִיּוֹן מִשְׁכַּן כְּבוֹדֶךָ, וְעַל מִזְבַּחֶךָ וְעַל הֵיכָלֶךָ. וּבְנֵה יְרוּשָׁלַיִם עִיר הַקֹּדֶשׁ בִּמְהֵרָה בְיָמֵינוּ, וְהַעֲלֵנוּ לְתוֹכָהּ, וְשַׂמְּחֵנוּ בְּבִנְיָנָהּ וְנֹאכַל מִפִּרְיָהּ וְנִשְׂבַּע מִטּוּבָהּ, וּנְבָרֶכְךָ עָלֶיהָ בִּקְדֻשָּׁה וּבְטָהֳרָה (בשבת וּרְצֵה וְהַחֲלִיצֵנוּ בְּיוֹם הַשַּׁבָּת הַזֶּה.) וְשַׂמְּחֵנוּ בְּיוֹם חַג הַמַּצּוֹת הַזֶּה. כִּי אַתָּה יְיָ טוֹב וּמֵטִיב לַכֹּל, וְנוֹדֶה לְךָ עַל הָאָרֶץ וְעַל פְּרִי הַגָּפֶן. בָּרוּךְ אַתָּה יְיָ, עַל הָאָרֶץ וְעַל פְּרִי הַגָּפֶן:

May Your Name *be praised forever, our King, the great and holy God and King in heaven and on earth. For You, Lord, our God and God of our fathers, forever befits song and praise, laud and hymn, strength and dominion, victory, greatness and might, glory, splendor, holiness and sovereignty; blessings and thanksgivings for now and forever. Blessed are You, Lord, Almighty God, King, great and extolled in praises, God of thanksgivings, Lord of wonders, who takes pleasure in songs of praise; King, God, the Life of all worlds.*

The following blessing is recited before drinking the fourth cup in a reclining position:

Blessed are You, Lord, our God, King of the universe, who creates the fruit of the vine.

After drinking the fourth cup, the concluding blessing is recited.
On Shabbat, include the passage in parentheses:

Blessed are You, Lord our God, King of the universe for the vine and the fruit of the vine, for the produce of the field, and for the precious, good and spacious land which You have favored to give as an inheritance to our fathers, to eat of its fruit and be satiated by its goodness. Have mercy, Lord our God, on Israel Your people, on Jerusalem Your city, on Zion the abode of Your glory, on Your altar and on Your Temple. Rebuild Jerusalem, the holy city, speedily in our days, and bring us up into it, and make us rejoice in its rebuilding, that we may eat of its fruit and be satiated by its goodness, and we will bless You in holiness and purity. (May it please You to strengthen us on this Shabbat day) and let us rejoice on this day of the Festival of Matzot. For You, Lord, are good and continually do good to all, and we thank You for the land and for the fruit of the vine. Blessed are You, Lord, for the land and for the fruit of the vine.

‏80 נִרְצָה ‏ca

חֲסַל סִדּוּר פֶּסַח כְּהִלְכָתוֹ, כְּכָל מִשְׁפָּטוֹ וְחֻקָּתוֹ. כַּאֲשֶׁר
זָכִינוּ לְסַדֵּר אוֹתוֹ, כֵּן נִזְכֶּה לַעֲשׂוֹתוֹ. זָךְ שׁוֹכֵן
מְעוֹנָה, קוֹמֵם קְהַל עֲדַת מִי מָנָה. בְּקָרוֹב נַהֵל נִטְעֵי כַנָּה,
פְּדוּיִם לְצִיּוֹן בְּרִנָּה.

לְשָׁנָה הַבָּאָה בִּירוּשָׁלָיִם:

‏80 סְפִירַת הָעֹמֶר ‏ca

For those making a second Seder: whoever did not count the *Omer* after *Maariv*
on the second night of Passover should count now.

הִנְנִי מוּכָן וּמְזֻמָּן לְקַיֵּם מִצְוַת עֲשֵׂה שֶׁל סְפִירַת הָעֹמֶר כְּמוֹ שֶׁכָּתוּב
בַּתּוֹרָה: וּסְפַרְתֶּם לָכֶם מִמָּחֳרַת הַשַּׁבָּת מִיּוֹם הֲבִיאֲכֶם אֶת עֹמֶר
הַתְּנוּפָה שֶׁבַע שַׁבָּתוֹת תְּמִימֹת תִּהְיֶינָה: עַד מִמָּחֳרַת הַשַּׁבָּת הַשְּׁבִיעִת
תִּסְפְּרוּ חֲמִשִּׁים יוֹם וְהִקְרַבְתֶּם מִנְחָה חֲדָשָׁה לַיְיָ:

בָּרוּךְ אַתָּה יְיָ אֱלֹהֵינוּ מֶלֶךְ הָעוֹלָם, אֲשֶׁר קִדְּשָׁנוּ בְּמִצְוֹתָיו
וְצִוָּנוּ עַל סְפִירַת הָעֹמֶר.

הַיּוֹם יוֹם אֶחָד לָעֹמֶר.

הָרַחֲמָן הוּא יַחֲזִיר לָנוּ עֲבוֹדַת בֵּית הַמִּקְדָּשׁ לִמְקוֹמָהּ,
בִּמְהֵרָה בְיָמֵינוּ אָמֵן סֶלָה.

ஐ *Nirtzah* ௐ

The Seder is now completed *in accordance with all of its laws, its ordinances and statutes. Just as we were found worthy to perform it, so may we be worthy to do so in the future. O pure one, who dwells on high, raise up the congregation that is without number. Soon may you guide the offshoots of Your plants to Zion, redeemed, with song.*

NEXT YEAR IN JERUSALEM!

ஐ *Counting the Omer* ௐ

For those making a second Seder: whoever did not count the *Omer* after *Maariv* on the second night of Passover should count now.

I am ready and prepared to perform the positive command concerning the Counting of the Omer, as it is written in the Torah: "You shall count from the day following the day of rest, from the day you brought the (Omer) sheaf of the wave-offering, seven whole weeks shall be counted, you shall count fifty days, to the day following the seventh week you shall count fifty days; and you shall offer a new offering to the Lord." (Vayikra 23:15–16)

Blessed are You, Lord our God, King of the Universe, who has sanctified us with His commandments and commanded us to count the Omer.

Today is the first day of the Omer.

The Compassionate One shall return the service of the Holy Temple for us, speedily in our days, Amen.

This song is for the first night of Pesach only.

‏&8 וּבְכֵן "וַיְהִי בַּחֲצִי הַלַּיְלָה" 80

אָז רוֹב נִסִּים הִפְלֵאתָ בַּלַּיְלָה, בְּרֹאשׁ אַשְׁמוּרוֹת זֶה הַלַּיְלָה,
גֵּר צֶדֶק נִצַּחְתּוֹ כְּנֶחֱלַק לוֹ לַיְלָה,   **וַיְהִי בַּחֲצִי הַלַּיְלָה.**

דַּנְתָּ מֶלֶךְ גְּרָר בַּחֲלוֹם הַלַּיְלָה, הִפְחַדְתָּ אֲרַמִּי בְּאֶמֶשׁ לַיְלָה,
וַיָּשַׂר יִשְׂרָאֵל לְמַלְאָךְ וַיּוּכַל לוֹ לַיְלָה,   **וַיְהִי בַּחֲצִי הַלַּיְלָה.**

זֶרַע בְּכוֹרֵי פַתְרוֹס מָחַצְתָּ בַּחֲצִי הַלַּיְלָה, חֵילָם לֹא מָצְאוּ בְּקוּמָם
בַּלַּיְלָה, **טִ**יסַת נְגִיד חֲרֹשֶׁת סִלִּיתָ בְּכוֹכְבֵי לַיְלָה,
וַיְהִי בַּחֲצִי הַלַּיְלָה.

יָעַץ מְחָרֵף לְנוֹפֵף אִוּוּי, הוֹבַשְׁתָּ פְגָרָיו בַּלַּיְלָה, **כָּרַע** בֵּל וּמַצָּבוֹ
בְּאִישׁוֹן לַיְלָה, **לְ**אִישׁ חֲמוּדוֹת נִגְלָה רָז חֲזוֹת לַיְלָה,
וַיְהִי בַּחֲצִי הַלַּיְלָה.

מִשְׁתַּכֵּר בִּכְלֵי קֹדֶשׁ נֶהֱרַג בּוֹ בַּלַּיְלָה, **נוֹשַׁע** מִבּוֹר אֲרָיוֹת פּוֹתֵר
בְּעִתוּתֵי לַיְלָה. **שִׂנְאָה** נָטַר אֲגָגִי וְכָתַב סְפָרִים לַיְלָה,
וַיְהִי בַּחֲצִי הַלַּיְלָה.

עוֹרַרְתָּ נִצְחֲךָ עָלָיו בְּנֶדֶד שְׁנַת לַיְלָה, **פּוּרָה** תִדְרוֹךְ לְשׁוֹמֵר מַה
מִּלַּיְלָה, **צָרַח** כַּשֹּׁמֵר וְשָׂח אָתָא בֹקֶר וְגַם לַיְלָה, **וַיְהִי בַּחֲצִי הַלַּיְלָה.**

קָרֵב יוֹם אֲשֶׁר הוּא לֹא יוֹם וְלֹא לַיְלָה, **רָם** הוֹדַע כִּי לְךָ הַיּוֹם אַף לְךָ
הַלַּיְלָה, **שׁוֹמְרִים** הַפְקֵד לְעִירְךָ כָּל הַיּוֹם וְכָל הַלַּיְלָה,
תָּאִיר כְּאוֹר יוֹם חֶשְׁכַּת לַיְלָה,   **וַיְהִי בַּחֲצִי הַלַּיְלָה:**

This song is for the first night of Pesach only.

❧ *And it came to pass at midnight!* ☙

Then, in times of old, You performed many wonders by night,
At the beginning of the watches of this night.
The righteous convert (Avraham)
You gave victory by dividing for him the night.

And it came to pass at midnight!

You judged the king of Gerar (Avimelech) in a dream at night.
You frightened the Aramean (Lavan) in the dark of the night.
Yisrael fought an angel and overcame him at night.

And it came to pass at midnight!

You crushed the firstborn of Patros (Egypt) at midnight.
They did not find their host upon arising at night.
The army of the prince of Charoset (Sisera) You swept away with the stars of the night.

And it came to pass at midnight!

The blasphemer (Sancheirev) planned to raise his hand against Jerusalem; but You made
him into dry corpses in the night.
Bel with its pedestal was overturned in the darkness of the night.
To the man You delighted in (Daniel) was revealed the secret of the visions of the night.

And it came to pass at midnight!

He who became drunk from the holy vessels (Belshazzar) was killed that very night.
Saved from the lion's den was he (Daniel) who interpreted the horrors of the night.
The Aggagi (Haman) nursed hatred and wrote edicts by night.

And it came to pass at midnight!

You began Your victory over him with disturbing (Achashveirosh's) sleep at night.|
Trample the winepress for those who ask the watchman, "What will come of the night?"
He will shout like a watchman, and say: "Morning shall came and also night."

And it came to pass at midnight!

Bring close the day that is neither day nor night.
Exalted One, make known that Yours is the day and Yours is also the night.
Appoint guards for Your city, all day and all night.
Brighten like the light of the day the darkness of night.

And it came to pass at midnight!

This song replaces the previous one on second Seder night.

‎אcontrols‎ וּבְכֵן "וַאֲמַרְתֶּם זֶבַח פֶּסַח" ‏

אֹמֶץ גְּבוּרוֹתֶיךָ הִפְלֵאתָ בַּפֶּסַח, **בְּ**רֹאשׁ כָּל מוֹעֲדוֹת נִשֵּׂאתָ פֶּסַח,
גִּלִּיתָ לְאֶזְרָחִי חֲצוֹת לֵיל פֶּסַח, ‏ ‏ ‏ ‏ ‏ ‏ ‏ ‏ ‏ ‏ ‏ וַאֲמַרְתֶּם זֶבַח פֶּסַח•

דְּלָתָיו דָּפַקְתָּ כְּחֹם הַיּוֹם בַּפֶּסַח, **הִ**סְעִיד נוֹצְצִים עֻגוֹת מַצּוֹת בַּפֶּסַח,
וְאֶל הַבָּקָר רָץ זֵכֶר לְשׁוֹר עֵרֶךְ פֶּסַח, ‏ ‏ ‏ ‏ ‏ ‏ וַאֲמַרְתֶּם זֶבַח פֶּסַח•

זֹעֲמוּ סְדוֹמִים וְלֹהֲטוּ בָּאֵשׁ בַּפֶּסַח, **חֻ**לַּץ לוֹט מֵהֶם, וּמַצּוֹת אָפָה בְּקֵץ
פֶּסַח, **טִ**אטֵאתָ אַדְמַת מֹף וְנֹף בְּעָבְרְךָ בַּפֶּסַח, ‏ ‏ ‏ וַאֲמַרְתֶּם זֶבַח פֶּסַח•

יָהּ, רֹאשׁ כָּל אוֹן מָחַצְתָּ בְּלֵיל שִׁמּוּר פֶּסַח, **כַּ**בִּיר, עַל בֵּן בְּכוֹר פָּסַחְתָּ
בְּדַם פֶּסַח, לְבִלְתִּי תֵּת מַשְׁחִית לָבֹא בִּפְתָחַי בַּפֶּסַח,
‏ וַאֲמַרְתֶּם זֶבַח פֶּסַח•

מְסֻגֶּרֶת סֻגָּרָה בְּעִתּוֹתֵי פֶּסַח, **נִ**שְׁמְדָה מִדְיָן בִּצְלִיל שְׂעוֹרֵי עֹמֶר פֶּסַח,
שֹׂרְפוּ מִשְׁמַנֵּי פּוּל וְלוּד בִּיקַד יְקוֹד פֶּסַח, ‏ ‏ ‏ ‏ ‏ וַאֲמַרְתֶּם זֶבַח פֶּסַח•

עוֹד הַיּוֹם בְּנֹב לַעֲמֹד, עַד גָּעָה עוֹנַת פֶּסַח, **פַּ**ס יָד כָּתְבָה לְקַעֲקֵעַ צוּל
בַּפֶּסַח, **צָ**פֹה הַצָּפִית עָרוֹךְ הַשֻּׁלְחָן, בַּפֶּסַח, ‏ ‏ ‏ ‏ וַאֲמַרְתֶּם זֶבַח פֶּסַח•

קָהָל כִּנְּסָה הֲדַסָּה צוֹם לְשַׁלֵּשׁ בַּפֶּסַח, **רֹ**אשׁ מִבֵּית רָשָׁע מָחַצְתָּ בְּעֵץ
חֲמִשִּׁים בַּפֶּסַח, **שְׁ**תֵּי אֵלֶּה רֶגַע, תָּבִיא לְעוּצִית בַּפֶּסַח,
תָּעֹז יָדְךָ וְתָרוּם יְמִינֶךָ, כְּלֵיל הִתְקַדֵּשׁ חַג פֶּסַח,
וַאֲמַרְתֶּם זֶבַח פֶּסַח•

This song replaces the previous one on second Seder night.

❦ *And you shall say: This is the Pesach sacrifice.* ❧

And you shall say: This is the Pesach sacrifice.
You displayed Your mighty powers wondrously on Pesach.
Above all seasons of delight You elevated Pesach.
You revealed the Exodus to the Oriental (Avraham) at the midnight of Pesach.
And you shall say: This is the Pesach sacrifice.

You knocked at his door in the heat of the day on Pesach.
He gave the angels cakes of matzah to dine on during Pesach.
He ran to the herd, harbinger of the sacrificial feast of the Pesach.
And you shall say: This is the Pesach sacrifice.

The Sodomites provoked and were burned up with fire on Pesach.
Lot was rescued from them and he baked Matzot at the end of Pesach.
You swept the ground of Moph and Noph (Egypt) when You passed though on Pesach.
And you shall say: This is the Pesach sacrifice.

God, You crushed the head of every firstborn on the watchful night of Pesach.
Powerful One, You skipped over Your firstborn by merit of the blood of Pesach.
So as not to let the Destroyer enter my threshold on Pesach.
And you shall say: This is the Pesach sacrifice.

The besieged city (Jericho) was besieged at the time of Pesach.
Midian was destroyed through a barley cake, from the Omer of Pesach.
The mighty nobles of Pul and Lud (Assyria) were burnt in a great conflagration on Pesach.
And you shall say: This is the Pesach sacrifice.

Still today (Sancheirev) would be standing at Nov until the time came for Pesach.
A hand inscribed the destruction of Tzul (Babylon) on Pesach.
As the watch was set, and the table on Pesach.
And you shall say: This is the Pesach sacrifice.

Hadassah (Esther) assembled a congregation for a three-day fast on Pesach.
The head of the wicked clan (Haman) You crushed, through a gallows of fifty cubits, on Pesach.
Double will You bring in an instant upon Utsis (Edom) on Pesach.
Let Your hand be strengthened and Your right arm be uplifted, as on that night when
You made holy the festival of Pesach.
And you shall say: This is the Pesach sacrifice.

ଔ כִּי לוֹ נָאֶה, כִּי לוֹ יָאֶה ଔ

אַדִּיר בִּמְלוּכָה, **בָּ**חוּר כַּהֲלָכָה, **גְּ**דוּדָיו יֹאמְרוּ לוֹ: לְךָ וּלְךָ, לְךָ כִּי
לְךָ, לְךָ אַף לְךָ, לְךָ יְיָ הַמַּמְלָכָה. **כִּי לוֹ נָאֶה, כִּי לוֹ יָאֶה.**

דָּגוּל בִּמְלוּכָה, **הָ**דוּר כַּהֲלָכָה, **וָ**תִיקָיו יֹאמְרוּ לוֹ: לְךָ וּלְךָ, לְךָ כִּי
לְךָ, לְךָ אַף לְךָ, לְךָ יְיָ הַמַּמְלָכָה. **כִּי לוֹ נָאֶה, כִּי לוֹ יָאֶה.**

זַכַּאי בִּמְלוּכָה, **חָ**סִין כַּהֲלָכָה, **טַ**פְסְרָיו יֹאמְרוּ לוֹ: לְךָ וּלְךָ, לְךָ כִּי
לְךָ, לְךָ אַף לְךָ, לְךָ יְיָ הַמַּמְלָכָה. **כִּי לוֹ נָאֶה, כִּי לוֹ יָאֶה.**

יָחִיד בִּמְלוּכָה, **כַּ**בִּיר כַּהֲלָכָה, **לִ**מּוּדָיו יֹאמְרוּ לוֹ: לְךָ וּלְךָ, לְךָ כִּי
לְךָ, לְךָ אַף לְךָ, לְךָ יְיָ הַמַּמְלָכָה. **כִּי לוֹ נָאֶה, כִּי לוֹ יָאֶה.**

מָרוֹם בִּמְלוּכָה, **נ**וֹרָא כַּהֲלָכָה, **ס**בִיבָיו יֹאמְרוּ לוֹ: לְךָ וּלְךָ, לְךָ כִּי
לְךָ, לְךָ אַף לְךָ, לְךָ יְיָ הַמַּמְלָכָה. **כִּי לוֹ נָאֶה, כִּי לוֹ יָאֶה.**

עָנָיו בִּמְלוּכָה, **פּ**וֹדֶה כַּהֲלָכָה, **צַ**דִּיקָיו יֹאמְרוּ לוֹ: לְךָ וּלְךָ, לְךָ כִּי
לְךָ, לְךָ אַף לְךָ, לְךָ יְיָ הַמַּמְלָכָה. **כִּי לוֹ נָאֶה, כִּי לוֹ יָאֶה.**

קָדוֹשׁ בִּמְלוּכָה, **רַ**חוּם כַּהֲלָכָה, **שׁ**נְאַנָּיו יֹאמְרוּ לוֹ: לְךָ וּלְךָ, לְךָ
כִּי לְךָ, לְךָ אַף לְךָ, לְךָ יְיָ הַמַּמְלָכָה. **כִּי לוֹ נָאֶה, כִּי לוֹ יָאֶה.**

תַּקִּיף בִּמְלוּכָה, **תּ**וֹמֵךְ כַּהֲלָכָה, **תְּ**מִימָיו יֹאמְרוּ לוֹ: לְךָ וּלְךָ, לְךָ
כִּי לְךָ, לְךָ אַף לְךָ, לְךָ יְיָ הַמַּמְלָכָה. **כִּי לוֹ נָאֶה, כִּי לוֹ יָאֶה.**

🙰 *To Him (praise) is becoming; to Him (praise) is fitting* 🙰

Mighty in Kingship, perfectly distinguished, His companies say to Him: to You and to You; to You, yes to You; to You, only to You; You, God, are the Sovereign.

To Him (praise) is becoming; to Him (praise) is fitting.

Renowned in kingship, perfectly glorious, His faithful say to Him: to You and to You; to You, yes to You; to You, only to You; You, God, are the Sovereign.

To Him (praise) is becoming; to Him (praise) is fitting.

Worthy in kingship, perfectly immune, His princes say to Him: to You and to You; to You, yes to You; to You, only to You; You, God, are the Sovereign.

To Him (praise) is becoming; to Him (praise) is fitting.

Unique in kingship, perfectly powerful, His learned ones say to Him: to You and to You; to You, yes to You; to You, only to You; You, God, are the Sovereign.

To Him (praise) is becoming; to Him (praise) is fitting.

Commanding in Kingship, perfectly awesome, His surrounding (angels) say to Him: to You and to You; to You, yes to You; to You, only to You; You, God, are the Sovereign.

To Him (praise) is becoming; to Him (praise) is fitting.

Modest in kingship, perfectly the Redeemer, His legions say to Him: to You and to You; to You, yes to You; to You, only to You; You, God, are the Sovereign.

To Him (praise) is becoming; to Him (praise) is fitting.

Holy in kingship, perfectly merciful, His snow-white angels say to Him: to You and to You; to You, yes to You; to You, only to You; You, God, are the Sovereign.

To Him (praise) is becoming; to Him (praise) is fitting.

Resolute in kingship, perfectly supportive, His perfect ones say to Him: to You and to You; to You, yes to You; to You, only to You; You, God, are the Sovereign.

To Him (praise) is becoming; to Him (praise) is fitting.

ﮒ אַדִּיר הוּא ﮒ

אַדִּיר הוּא,
יִבְנֶה בֵיתוֹ בְּקָרוֹב, בִּמְהֵרָה בִּמְהֵרָה, בְּיָמֵינוּ בְּקָרוֹב.
אֵל בְּנֵה, אֵל בְּנֵה, בְּנֵה בֵיתְךָ בְּקָרוֹב.

בָּחוּר הוּא, גָּדוֹל הוּא, דָּגוּל הוּא,
יִבְנֶה בֵיתוֹ בְּקָרוֹב, בִּמְהֵרָה בִּמְהֵרָה, בְּיָמֵינוּ בְּקָרוֹב.
אֵל בְּנֵה, אֵל בְּנֵה, בְּנֵה בֵיתְךָ בְּקָרוֹב.

הָדוּר הוּא, וָתִיק הוּא, זַכַּאי הוּא, חָסִיד הוּא,
יִבְנֶה בֵיתוֹ בְּקָרוֹב, בִּמְהֵרָה בִּמְהֵרָה, בְּיָמֵינוּ בְּקָרוֹב.
אֵל בְּנֵה, אֵל בְּנֵה, בְּנֵה בֵיתְךָ בְּקָרוֹב.

טָהוֹר הוּא, יָחִיד הוּא, כַּבִּיר הוּא, לָמוּד הוּא, מֶלֶךְ הוּא,
נוֹרָא הוּא, סַגִּיב הוּא, עִזּוּז הוּא, פּוֹדֶה הוּא, צַדִּיק הוּא,
יִבְנֶה בֵיתוֹ בְּקָרוֹב, בִּמְהֵרָה בִּמְהֵרָה, בְּיָמֵינוּ בְּקָרוֹב.
אֵל בְּנֵה, אֵל בְּנֵה, בְּנֵה בֵיתְךָ בְּקָרוֹב.

קָדוֹשׁ הוּא, רַחוּם הוּא, שַׁדַּי הוּא, תַּקִּיף הוּא,
יִבְנֶה בֵיתוֹ בְּקָרוֹב, בִּמְהֵרָה בִּמְהֵרָה, בְּיָמֵינוּ בְּקָרוֹב.
אֵל בְּנֵה, אֵל בְּנֵה, בְּנֵה בֵיתְךָ בְּקָרוֹב.

ಬ He is mighty ಲ

He is mighty.
May He soon rebuild His House, speedily, yes speedily, in our days, soon.
God, rebuild, God, rebuild, rebuild Your House soon!

He is distinguished, He is great, He is renowned.
May He soon rebuild His House, speedily, yes speedily, in our days, soon.
God, rebuild, God, rebuild, rebuild Your House soon!

He is glorious, He is faithful, He is worthy, He is gracious.
May He soon rebuild His House, speedily, yes speedily, in our days, soon.
God, rebuild, God, rebuild, rebuild Your House soon!

He is pure, He is unique, He is powerful, He is majestic, He is awesome,
He is sublime, He is all-powerful, He is the Redeemer, He is righteous.
May He soon rebuild His House, speedily, yes speedily, in our days, soon.
God, rebuild, God, rebuild, rebuild Your House soon!

He is holy, He is merciful, He is Almighty, He is forceful.
May He soon rebuild His House, speedily, yes speedily, in our days, soon.
God, rebuild, God, rebuild, rebuild Your House soon!

‏8 אֶחָד מִי יוֹדֵעַ? ‏3

אֶחָד מִי יוֹדֵעַ? **אֶחָד אֲנִי יוֹדֵעַ:** אֶחָד אֱלֹהֵינוּ שֶׁבַּשָּׁמַיִם וּבָאָרֶץ.

שְׁנַיִם מִי יוֹדֵעַ? שְׁנַיִם אֲנִי יוֹדֵעַ: שְׁנֵי לֻחוֹת הַבְּרִית, אֶחָד אֱלֹהֵינוּ שֶׁבַּשָּׁמַיִם וּבָאָרֶץ.

שְׁלֹשָׁה מִי יוֹדֵעַ? שְׁלֹשָׁה אֲנִי יוֹדֵעַ: שְׁלֹשָׁה אָבוֹת, שְׁנֵי לֻחוֹת הַבְּרִית, אֶחָד אֱלֹהֵינוּ שֶׁבַּשָּׁמַיִם וּבָאָרֶץ.

אַרְבַּע מִי יוֹדֵעַ? אַרְבַּע אֲנִי יוֹדֵעַ: אַרְבַּע אִמָּהוֹת, שְׁלֹשָׁה אָבוֹת, שְׁנֵי לֻחוֹת הַבְּרִית, אֶחָד אֱלֹהֵינוּ שֶׁבַּשָּׁמַיִם וּבָאָרֶץ.

חֲמִשָּׁה מִי יוֹדֵעַ? חֲמִשָּׁה אֲנִי יוֹדֵעַ: חֲמִשָּׁה חוּמְשֵׁי תוֹרָה, אַרְבַּע אִמָּהוֹת, שְׁלֹשָׁה אָבוֹת, שְׁנֵי לֻחוֹת הַבְּרִית, אֶחָד אֱלֹהֵינוּ שֶׁבַּשָּׁמַיִם וּבָאָרֶץ.

שִׁשָּׁה מִי יוֹדֵעַ? שִׁשָּׁה אֲנִי יוֹדֵעַ: שִׁשָּׁה סִדְרֵי מִשְׁנָה, חֲמִשָּׁה חוּמְשֵׁי תוֹרָה, אַרְבַּע אִמָּהוֹת, שְׁלֹשָׁה אָבוֹת, שְׁנֵי לֻחוֹת הַבְּרִית, אֶחָד אֱלֹהֵינוּ שֶׁבַּשָּׁמַיִם וּבָאָרֶץ.

שִׁבְעָה מִי יוֹדֵעַ? שִׁבְעָה אֲנִי יוֹדֵעַ: שִׁבְעָה יְמֵי שַׁבַּתָּא, שִׁשָּׁה סִדְרֵי מִשְׁנָה, חֲמִשָּׁה חוּמְשֵׁי תוֹרָה, אַרְבַּע אִמָּהוֹת, שְׁלֹשָׁה אָבוֹת, שְׁנֵי לֻחוֹת הַבְּרִית, אֶחָד אֱלֹהֵינוּ שֶׁבַּשָּׁמַיִם וּבָאָרֶץ.

שְׁמוֹנָה מִי יוֹדֵעַ? שְׁמוֹנָה אֲנִי יוֹדֵעַ: שְׁמוֹנָה יְמֵי מִילָה, שִׁבְעָה יְמֵי שַׁבַּתָּא, שִׁשָּׁה סִדְרֵי מִשְׁנָה, חֲמִשָּׁה חוּמְשֵׁי תוֹרָה, אַרְבַּע אִמָּהוֹת, שְׁלֹשָׁה אָבוֹת, שְׁנֵי לֻחוֹת הַבְּרִית, אֶחָד אֱלֹהֵינוּ שֶׁבַּשָּׁמַיִם וּבָאָרֶץ.

∾ *Who knows one?* ൙

Who knows one? I know one: *One is our God, in heaven and on earth.*

Who knows two? I know two: *two are the Tablets of Covenant; One is our God, in heaven and on earth.*

Who knows three? I know three: *three are the Patriarchs; two are the Tablets of Covenant; One is our God, in heaven and on earth.*

Who knows four? I know four: *four are the Matriarchs; three are the Patriarchs; two are the Tablets of Covenant; One is our God, in heaven and on earth.*

Who knows five? I know five: *five are the Books of the Torah; four are the Matriarchs; three are the Patriarchs; two are the Tablets of Covenant; One is our God, in heaven and on earth.*

Who knows six? I know six: *six are the Orders of the Mishnah; five are the Books of the Torah; four are the Matriarchs; three are the Patriarchs; two are the Tablets of Covenant; One is our God, in heaven and on earth.*

Who knows seven? I know seven: *seven are the days of the week; six are the Orders of the Mishnah; five are the Books of the Torah; four are the Matriarchs; three are the Patriarchs; two are the Tablets of Covenant; One is our God, in heaven and on earth.*

Who knows eight? *I know eight: eight are the days to circumcision; seven are the days of the week; six are the Orders of the Mishnah; five are the Books of the Torah; four are the Matriarchs; three are the Patriarchs; two are the Tablets of Covenant; One is our God, in heaven and on earth.*

תִּשְׁעָה מִי יוֹדֵעַ? תִּשְׁעָה אֲנִי יוֹדֵעַ: תִּשְׁעָה יַרְחֵי לֵדָה, שְׁמוֹנָה יְמֵי מִילָה, שִׁבְעָה יְמֵי שַׁבַּתָּא, שִׁשָּׁה סִדְרֵי מִשְׁנָה, חֲמִשָּׁה חוּמְשֵׁי תּוֹרָה, אַרְבַּע אִמָּהוֹת, שְׁלֹשָׁה אָבוֹת, שְׁנֵי לֻחוֹת הַבְּרִית, אֶחָד אֱלֹהֵינוּ שֶׁבַּשָּׁמַיִם וּבָאָרֶץ.

עֲשָׂרָה מִי יוֹדֵעַ? עֲשָׂרָה אֲנִי יוֹדֵעַ: עֲשָׂרָה דִבְּרַיָּא, תִּשְׁעָה יַרְחֵי לֵדָה, שְׁמוֹנָה יְמֵי מִילָה, שִׁבְעָה יְמֵי שַׁבַּתָּא, שִׁשָּׁה סִדְרֵי מִשְׁנָה, חֲמִשָּׁה חוּמְשֵׁי תּוֹרָה, אַרְבַּע אִמָּהוֹת, שְׁלֹשָׁה אָבוֹת, שְׁנֵי לֻחוֹת הַבְּרִית, אֶחָד אֱלֹהֵינוּ שֶׁבַּשָּׁמַיִם וּבָאָרֶץ.

אַחַד עָשָׂר מִי יוֹדֵעַ? אַחַד עָשָׂר אֲנִי יוֹדֵעַ: אַחַד עָשָׂר כּוֹכְבַיָּא, עֲשָׂרָה דִבְּרַיָּא, תִּשְׁעָה יַרְחֵי לֵדָה, שְׁמוֹנָה יְמֵי מִילָה, שִׁבְעָה יְמֵי שַׁבַּתָּא, שִׁשָּׁה סִדְרֵי מִשְׁנָה, חֲמִשָּׁה חוּמְשֵׁי תּוֹרָה, אַרְבַּע אִמָּהוֹת, שְׁלֹשָׁה אָבוֹת, שְׁנֵי לֻחוֹת הַבְּרִית, אֶחָד אֱלֹהֵינוּ שֶׁבַּשָּׁמַיִם וּבָאָרֶץ.

שְׁנֵים עָשָׂר מִי יוֹדֵעַ? שְׁנֵים עָשָׂר אֲנִי יוֹדֵעַ: שְׁנֵים עָשָׂר שִׁבְטַיָּא, אַחַד עָשָׂר כּוֹכְבַיָּא, עֲשָׂרָה דִבְּרַיָּא, תִּשְׁעָה יַרְחֵי לֵדָה, שְׁמוֹנָה יְמֵי מִילָה, שִׁבְעָה יְמֵי שַׁבַּתָּא, שִׁשָּׁה סִדְרֵי מִשְׁנָה, חֲמִשָּׁה חוּמְשֵׁי תּוֹרָה, אַרְבַּע אִמָּהוֹת, שְׁלֹשָׁה אָבוֹת, שְׁנֵי לֻחוֹת הַבְּרִית, אֶחָד אֱלֹהֵינוּ שֶׁבַּשָּׁמַיִם וּבָאָרֶץ.

שְׁלֹשָׁה עָשָׂר מִי יוֹדֵעַ? שְׁלֹשָׁה עָשָׂר אֲנִי יוֹדֵעַ: שְׁלֹשָׁה עָשָׂר מִדַּיָּא, שְׁנֵים עָשָׂר שִׁבְטַיָּא, אַחַד עָשָׂר כּוֹכְבַיָּא, עֲשָׂרָה דִבְּרַיָּא, תִּשְׁעָה יַרְחֵי לֵדָה, שְׁמוֹנָה יְמֵי מִילָה, שִׁבְעָה יְמֵי שַׁבַּתָּא, שִׁשָּׁה סִדְרֵי מִשְׁנָה, חֲמִשָּׁה חוּמְשֵׁי תּוֹרָה, אַרְבַּע אִמָּהוֹת, שְׁלֹשָׁה אָבוֹת, שְׁנֵי לֻחוֹת הַבְּרִית, אֶחָד אֱלֹהֵינוּ שֶׁבַּשָּׁמַיִם וּבָאָרֶץ.

Who knows nine? I know nine: *nine are the months of the pregnancy; eight are the days to circumcision; seven are the days of the week; six are the Orders of the Mishnah; five are the Books of the Torah; four are the Matriarchs; three are the Patriarchs; two are the Tablets of Covenant; One is our God, in heaven and on earth.*

Who knows ten? I know ten: *ten are the Ten Commandments; nine are the months of the pregnancy; eight are the days to circumcision; seven are the days of the week; six are the Orders of the Mishnah; five are the Books of the Torah; four are the Matriarchs; three are the Patriarchs; two are the Tablets of Covenant; One is our God, in heaven and on earth.*

Who knows eleven? I know eleven: *eleven are the stars (in Yosef's dream); ten are the Ten Commandments; nine are the months of the pregnancy; eight are the days to circumcision; seven are the days of the week; six are the Orders of the Mishnah; five are the Books of the Torah; four are the Matriarchs; three are the Patriarchs; two are the Tablets of Covenant; One is our God, in heaven and on earth.*

Who knows twelve? I know twelve: *twelve are the tribes (of Israel); eleven are the stars (in Yosef's dream); ten are the Ten Commandments; nine are the months of the pregnancy; eight are the days to circumcision; seven are the days of the week; six are the Orders of the Mishnah; five are the Books of the Torah; four are the Matriarchs; three are the Patriarchs; two are the Tablets of Covenant; One is our God, in heaven and on earth.*

Who knows thirteen? I know thirteen: *thirteen are the attributes of God; twelve are the tribes (of Israel); eleven are the stars (in Yosef's dream); ten are the Ten Commandments; nine are the months of the pregnancy; eight are the days to circumcision; seven are the days of the week; six are the Orders of the Mishnah; five are the Books of the Torah; four are the Matriarchs; three are the Patriarchs; two are the Tablets of Covenant; One is our God, in heaven and on earth.*

‫ﬠ   חַד גַּדְיָא, חַד גַּדְיָא   ﬠ‬

חַד גַּדְיָא, חַד גַּדְיָא,
דְּזַבִּין אַבָּא בִּתְרֵי זוּזֵי,
חַד גַּדְיָא, חַד גַּדְיָא.

וְאָתָא שׁוּנְרָא,
וְאָכְלָה לְגַדְיָא,
דְּזַבִּין אַבָּא בִּתְרֵי זוּזֵי,
חַד גַּדְיָא, חַד גַּדְיָא.

וְאָתָא כַלְבָּא, וְנָשַׁךְ לְשׁוּנְרָא,
דְּאָכְלָה לְגַדְיָא,
דְּזַבִּין אַבָּא בִּתְרֵי זוּזֵי,
חַד גַּדְיָא, חַד גַּדְיָא.

וְאָתָא חוּטְרָא, וְהִכָּה לְכַלְבָּא,
דְּנָשַׁךְ לְשׁוּנְרָא, דְּאָכְלָה לְגַדְיָא,
דְּזַבִּין אַבָּא בִּתְרֵי זוּזֵי,
חַד גַּדְיָא, חַד גַּדְיָא.

וְאָתָא נוּרָא, וְשָׂרַף לְחוּטְרָא,
דְּהִכָּה לְכַלְבָּא, דְּנָשַׁךְ לְשׁוּנְרָא,
דְּאָכְלָה לְגַדְיָא,
דְּזַבִּין אַבָּא בִּתְרֵי זוּזֵי,
חַד גַּדְיָא, חַד גַּדְיָא.

וְאָתָא מַיָּא, וְכָבָה לְנוּרָא,
דְּשָׂרַף לְחוּטְרָא, דְּהִכָּה לְכַלְבָּא,
דְּנָשַׁךְ לְשׁוּנְרָא, דְּאָכְלָה לְגַדְיָא,
דְּזַבִּין אַבָּא בִּתְרֵי זוּזֵי,
חַד גַּדְיָא, חַד גַּדְיָא.

וְאָתָא תוֹרָא, וְשָׁתָא לְמַיָּא,
דְּכָבָה לְנוּרָא, דְּשָׂרַף לְחוּטְרָא,
דְּהִכָּה לְכַלְבָּא, דְּנָשַׁךְ לְשׁוּנְרָא,
דְּאָכְלָה לְגַדְיָא,
דְּזַבִּין אַבָּא בִּתְרֵי זוּזֵי,
חַד גַּדְיָא, חַד גַּדְיָא.

וְאָתָא הַשּׁוֹחֵט, וְשָׁחַט לְתוֹרָא,
דְּשָׁתָא לְמַיָּא, דְּכָבָה לְנוּרָא,
דְּשָׂרַף לְחוּטְרָא, דְּהִכָּה לְכַלְבָּא,
דְּנָשַׁךְ לְשׁוּנְרָא, דְּאָכְלָה לְגַדְיָא,
דְּזַבִּין אַבָּא בִּתְרֵי זוּזֵי,
חַד גַּדְיָא, חַד גַּדְיָא.

וְאָתָא מַלְאַךְ הַמָּוֶת, וְשָׁחַט לְשׁוֹחֵט,
דְּשָׁחַט לְתוֹרָא, דְּשָׁתָא לְמַיָּא,
דְּכָבָה לְנוּרָא, דְּשָׂרַף לְחוּטְרָא,
דְּהִכָּה לְכַלְבָּא, דְּנָשַׁךְ לְשׁוּנְרָא,
דְּאָכְלָה לְגַדְיָא,
דְּזַבִּין אַבָּא בִּתְרֵי זוּזֵי,
חַד גַּדְיָא, חַד גַּדְיָא.

וְאָתָא הַקָּדוֹשׁ בָּרוּךְ הוּא, וְשָׁחַט
לְמַלְאַךְ הַמָּוֶת, דְּשָׁחַט לְתוֹרָא,
דְּשָׁתָא לְמַיָּא, דְּכָבָה לְנוּרָא,
דְּשָׂרַף לְחוּטְרָא, דְּהִכָּה לְכַלְבָּא,
דְּנָשַׁךְ לְשׁוּנְרָא, דְּאָכְלָה לְגַדְיָא,
דְּזַבִּין אַבָּא בִּתְרֵי זוּזֵי,
חַד גַּדְיָא, חַד גַּדְיָא.

ʚɔ *One little goat* ෬

One little goat, one little goat,
that father bought for two zuzim,
one little goat, one little goat.

And then came a cat
and ate that goat
that father bought for two zuzim,
one little goat, one little goat.

And then came a dog
and bit the cat,
that ate the goat
that father bought for two zuzim,
one little goat, one little goat.

And then came a stick
and beat the dog,
that bit the cat,
that ate the goat that father bought
for two zuzim,
one little goat, one little goat.

And then came a fire
and burnt the stick,
that beat the dog,
that bit the cat,
that ate the goat
that father bought for two zuzim,
one little goat, one little goat.

And then came some water
and put out the fire,
that burnt the stick,
that beat the dog,
that bit the cat,
that ate the goat
that father bought for two zuzim,
one little goat, one little goat.

And then came an ox
and drank the water,
that put out the fire,
that burnt the stick, that beat the dog,
that bit the cat, that ate the goat
that father bought for two zuzim,
one little goat, one little goat.

And then came a slaughterer
and slaughtered the ox,
that drank the water,
that put out the fire,
that burnt the stick, that beat the dog,
that bit the cat, that ate the goat
that father bought for two zuzim,
one little goat, one little goat.

And then came the angel of death
and slew the slaughter,
who slaughtered the ox,
that drank the water, that put out the fire,
that burnt the stick, that beat the dog,
that bit the cat, that ate the goat
that father bought for two zuzim,
one little goat, one little goat.

And then came the Holy One,
blessed be He,
and killed the angel of death,
who slew the slaughterer,
who slaughtered the ox,
that drank the water,
that put out the fire,
that burnt the stick, that beat the dog,
that bit the cat, that ate the goat
that father bought for two zuzim,
one little goat, one little goat.

Nechama Remembered :דברי זכרון

A MEMORIAL TRIBUTE TO
NECHAMA LEIBOWITZ זצ"ל

On the fifth of *Nissan*, we commemorate the *yahrzeit* of our revered teacher, Nechama Leibowitz זצ"ל.

The Master Teacher

Nechama requested that on her gravestone she be identified simply as "*morah*," a teacher. It is a characteristically simple epitaph, but in Nechama's case it speaks volumes. Certainly, Nechama stands out as one of the master teachers of Torah in our generation, both in terms of her academic writings and her insights on pedagogy. But, perhaps, the most important quality that identified Nechama as a teacher was the relationship that she established with her students. One could not sit anonymously in Nechama's *shiurim*. She demanded that each student write the answers to her questions. She checked them all on the spot and gave responses. Thus, she got to know her students. Similarly, her *Gilyonot* were distributed far and wide. Literally thousands of students would send their answers in to Nechama by mail. She would examine them all personally and respond. Nechama was a favorite of the Israeli Postal Service.

Respect for the Common Person

Even by mail, Nechama became acquainted with her students. It happened once that she received answers to the *Gilyonot* on a weekly basis from an unidentified respondent. Curious as to who this dedicated student might be, Nechama eventually asked that she identify herself. It turned out that the correspondent was a waitress from Ashkelon. Nechama could count among her students some of the accomplished rabbis and educators of our generation. She rarely spoke about them, but she loved to mention the waitress from Ashkelon. She was truly gratified and inspired by the dedication of the common people to Torah study and Judaism.

Only in Israel

Nechama similarly took pride in the Torah knowledge and religious sentiment of the "man on the street" in Israel. These qualities often manifested themselves in encounters on Israeli buses and taxis. Nechama loved to recount these stories. The following are two of her favorites:

ॐ An older gentleman boarded a rather full bus, and a young boy stood up to offer his seat. The man said to the boy: "Because of which part of the verse did you stand up for me?" (The man was referring to the verse in *Vayikra* 19:32 which states that one should rise before the elderly and honor the aged. The commentators indicate that one reference is to the elderly and one is to the wise.) The boy responded: "Both." And then the man took the seat. Nechama always ended the story with a smile, stating: "And nobody had to say which verse they were referring to!"

ॐ One Friday, Nechama got into a taxi outside a hotel. The concierge came out and told the driver that he had a guest who wanted to travel the next day (Shabbat) to Haifa for a very good fare. The driver declined, and the concierge tried to entice him by increasing the fare. The driver was clearly not wealthy, but he continued to refuse until he finally got angry with the concierge and left. For the entire ride, the cab driver kept muttering under his breath: "I don't travel on Shabbat. I don't travel on Shabbat. I don't travel on Shabbat! On Shabbat I go to the Beit Knesset to be with God!" In telling the story, Nechama would repeat the last line several times. She was struck by the purity of this simple man's religious sentiment.

Love of the Land, the People, and the State

Nechama settled in Israel before the establishment of the state. Her bus stories also included tales of journeys from Tel Aviv to Jerusalem under armed attack before the state was established. She took great pride in the accomplishments of *Bnai Yisrael* in the State of Israel. Once again, it was the special sense of caring that most impressed Nechama. Following Operation Shlomo in which 14,000 Ethiopians were brought to Israel in one weekend, Nechama could not stop marveling at the fact that "each of them had a place to sleep." Nechama was troubled when she observed a lack of such caring. She entered the hospital for the first time in her life when she was 87 years old. When visiting her in the hospital, she expressed her dismay that the doctors could talk to each other about the patients as if the patients were not there. This was antithetical to Nechama, the teacher. This certainly shouldn't happen in a Jewish hospital.

Nechama's love of *Eretz Yisrael* and *Medinat Yisrael* was so strong that she could not be persuaded to leave the country. Many times, her students wanted her to come to *Chutz La'aretz* to train teachers. She never agreed to leave Israel, even for such an important purpose.

"The Honor of the King's Daughter is Within"

Nechama's ability to respect and value others was a reflection of her deep humility. Many in her position might have developed a sense of self-importance. Nechama truly did not recognize her own greatness. I once received a call from Yitshak Reiner, the editor of Nechama's *Gilyonot*, from Nechama's apartment. When Nechama got on the phone, she said: "Shmuel, do you remember me?"

Nechama lived in a very modest two-room apartment. Her walls were lined with the *Gilyonot* that she had produced over the years. She could not be convinced to take a gift. Her students often tried unsuccessfully to devise a method of giving her a gift as a token of their appreciation. The only thing that I ever saw her accept were candies that she could place on her table to pass around to the students during *shiurim*. Nechama did not make her Torah study a vehicle for self-aggrandizement on either a financial or a psychological level. She embodied the Mishna from *Pirke Avot*: "If you have learned much Torah do not ascribe greatness to yourself, because for that purpose you were created." (*Avot* 2:9)

An Honest Encounter with the Text

It was perhaps Nechama's humility as well that enabled her to be the outstanding Torah scholar that she was. She came to learn Torah from the great medieval commentators. She came to hear them speak, not to have them speak for her. It was this sense of honest scholarship that she imparted to her students; and in turn it was this sense of humility that endeared her to them.

Her gravestone reads simply "*morah.*" That is her legacy. The fact that her *Gilyonot* are still utilized, that her Torah is still learned, is the greatest and most meaningful memorial that could be established for Nechama, our *morah.*

Nechama did not leave any children to say *kaddish* for her. She did, however, leave a host of students to remember her and pray for the ascent of her soul. May her soul be bound up in the bond of life.

Shmuel Peerless
ה׳ ניסן תש״ס

Index of Sources from Nechama Leibowitz' Gilyonot and Other Works

Devarim 26:6
And they were evil toward us: Ki Tavo 5709
Let us deal wisely: Shemot 5711
They will escape from the land: Shemot 5728
And they placed taskmasters: Shemot 5730
And they built store cities: Ekev 5724
Pitom and Ramses: Shemot 5730
With rigor: Shemot 5718; question 4—editors
Anecdote: relating to Shemot 5715

Devarim 26:7
And the king of Egypt died: Shemot 5718
Shemot 2:23–25: Miketz 5711
Our burden: Toldot 5711
And our oppression: Mishpatim 5716

Devarim 26:8
At Midnight: Bo 5727
To take for himself a nation: Ve'etchanan 5721
The staff: Beshalach 5730
Pairs of Plagues: Editors' question based on Bo 5724—Study Guide

The Ten Plagues
The Purpose of the Plagues:
1–2) Va'era 5713
3) Editors' question based on *Rashi's Commentary on the Torah*, p. 460
4) Va'era 5721
5) Va'era 5713
The Hardening of Pharoah's Heart: Va'era 5718
Rabbi Yehuda's Acronym: Bo 5724

At The Sea They Were Struck: Va'era 5715, 5721; questions 3–4—editors

It Would Have Been Enough: Yitro 5710

Because G-d Passed Over: Bo 5717; question 4—Bo 5707

This Matzah That We Eat: Bo 5720; question 3—editors

Chag Hapesach: Emor 5709

This Bitter Herb That We Eat: Based on Bo 5727

In Every Generation: Bo 5718; Harav Kook—Bo 5716

INDEX OF COMMENTATORS CITED

INDEX TO RABBINIC SOURCES CITED

SAGES — TANNAIM AND AMORAIM

Rabbi Yitshak Reiner studied with Nechama Leibowitz for many years, and is currently involved in the publication of her *Gilyonot* along with study guides and suggested answers. He has served as the director of the Department for Seminars and Advanced Courses in the Department of Education of the Jewish Agency in Jerusalem, and was also the principal of the Tahkemoni Jewish Day School in Antwerp, Belgium.

Rabbi Shmuel Peerless is the director of the Center for Jewish School Leadership at Bar-Ilan University's Lookstein Center. Previously, he served as the educational director of the Hillel Academy of Dayton, Ohio and the Hebrew Academy of Montreal, and was the director of the World Council for Torah Education. He studied with Nechama Leibowitz for several years, and has written *To Study and to Teach: The Methodology of Nechama Leibowitz*, which is scheduled for publication.